To Pat

thank you for

being my.

friend.

x x x

IN MY OWN WORDS

My Life From 1934 to 2019

Faith Sonia Richards

For my darling Rosie May

Always there for me…

and her son Geo, who idolised his Grandad

1

In 1934, my mother found herself in a bit of a predicament. Mum had two older children and another one on the way. She had just found out that her husband, my Dad, had committed bigamy with one of my mother's own cousins, and she was now also pregnant by my Dad. This is when Mum gave birth to me. She said I was born in the Workhouse! That was just before it had closed and became the Newton Abbot Maternity Unit. Mum said it was the only place she could go and take the other two children, because she had no-one to leave them with at that time.

I was born in the November of 1934. Mum called me Faith Sonia. I was then introduced to my brother Colin John, born in August 1931 and my sister April Cora, born April 1933. I didn't know then how important they were to be in my life and the bond that was going to grow between us three.

We all came back to Teignmouth not realising how beautiful and wonderful a place it was to be brought up in. All I could think of was growing up here and how lucky we were, with the soft sands and sea, the river Teign and green fields all around. What a lovely playground. We were very poor, but God had blessed us with this wonderful friendly town.

Now I sit here in my eighties, writing my memoirs, overlooking the river Teign and Teign Street where I would play as a child. I can still picture us in our swimsuits running through Sun Lane to go for a swim on the quay at high tide. I am reflecting on what my Mum told me before I could remember for myself. She told me that I was about three months old and was very ill with whooping cough and shingles, and not expected to pull through. People said I couldn't have had shingles if I had not had chickenpox, but I did, and I had shingles again later in my seventies. Mum also told me we lived in Clampet Lane where my brother Theodore (Theo), was born in 1936. I would have been one year and ten months then. Mum must have forgiven Dad, but their marriage was a stormy one, as Dad was always leaving.

But she stood by him when he was brought to trial at Court for bigamy. He didn't go to prison.

Mum told me that when I was about two years old, I went to Sunday school. When I was young you had to call adults Auntie or Uncle or Mr. or Mrs. and their surnames, so my Sunday school teacher was known as Auntie Violet. She would pick me up from home and take me in my pushchair every Sunday morning and afternoon to the Salvation Army. I remembered the little Bible stories being taught in the baby class in a big sand tray with little figures and a mirror for water. Later we could take part by placing some of the figures like Joseph in the well. Then we would sing, 'Jesus Wants Me for A Sunbeam', or 'Zacchaeus Was A Very Little Man', I remember all the little songs we were taught, and I sang them to my own children, when they were little.

April and I sang in the Salvation Army choir when we were older as we both loved to sing. At a very early age I seemed to have great faith, which saw me through the hard times of my life. The things I was taught at Sunday school never left me. Mum made April and me leave the Salvation Army in our teens because they asked if we would wear the Salvation Army uniform. Mum said no and sent us to another church but April and I never liked it, because looking back on it now, some of the people looked down on us because we were so poorly dressed, and we could see they didn't want us there. We missed the Salvation Army for our singing and evening recreations. We did love it there so we ran the streets instead.

Let's get back to the memories. I am running away with myself. We seemed to have moved a lot. When I was coming up to three years old, somewhere about 1937, we moved to Willow Street. Gran Richards, my Dad's Mum, took me to a jumble sale and bought me a little dolly. Her little blue eyes would open and close. I had never had a toy before as Mum could barely feed us, so I thought I would show my dolly to my friend Margaret in the next street, who I played with at times. She poked her eyes out and I went home crying.

The other thing I remembered at Willow Street was my Dad. He was so caring and loving towards me when I had a nasty boil come up on my knee and got a hot bottle to draw it out. Dad was telling me

8

what he was doing, and it would hurt. I remember my Dad speaking to me gently to comfort me and telling me what a big girl I was. He gave me a big hug then dressed my knee. It's funny how I remember. Although I don't remember my Dad being around much, he was always kind to me.

One day I was talking to Mum about Willow Street and she wondered how I could remember this as she said I wasn't three years old at that time, so I gave her a description of the room even to which side of the big scrubbed white table top Dad sat me on. I can still picture that room and my Dad standing there with me until this day, a sweet memory now.

The next thing I remember was going to stay with my Gran Stevenson, my Mum's Mum at Newton Abbot. I was still only in my third year and the first thing I did wrong was to laugh at my Grandad. He walked around my chair, said good night and walked across the floor to the door that led upstairs. As he began to crawl up the stairs, I thought he was playing games with me and I laughed, but Gran was very cross with me and told me not to laugh at a blind man. I didn't know what she meant.

Next morning, I came down for breakfast, and on my plate was something called chitterlings. I took one look at this greasy mass on my plate and I knew I couldn't eat them without being sick. Gran Stevenson was very disapproving of me for turning my nose up at good food, so it was put in front of me again at dinner time, and then at teatime, and again the following morning for my breakfast. Now what was I going to do? I hadn't had anything to eat for over a day, and if I had eaten it, I was sure to be ill. I couldn't eat greasy food. So, I asked if I could be excused to leave the table as I needed the toilet.

There was a block of toilets outside in a courtyard, shared by all the little cottages around there. As I sat on the toilet, I thought what can I do? I knew I couldn't eat the chitterlings, if I did I would be sick, then I remembered that my Aunt Paula, my Mum's sister, was living not far away from Gran Stevenson. So off I went.

I remembered to walk towards the tower, 'now which way do I go?' I looked up and down the streets and I happened to pick the right street and turned into East Street. Now I had to look for some steep steps. There were a hundred and thirteen steps to Aunt Paula's house. I counted them many times after, although I couldn't count at this time. I don't know how many times I had been brought to Newton Abbot to remember what I did, but I managed to pick the wrong set of steps. I should have gone a little more down East Street. But still I carried on up this set of steps. When I got to the top, I knew I had gone wrong, because Aunt Paula's house wasn't there.

I looked around me and thought 'where do I go from here?' I turned left and started to walk up the road. Why? I didn't have a clue. So, I just carried on up the road. After what seemed a very long time I got to a gate. I climbed up this gate so I could see better and at the bottom of this field I saw a brown wooden hut. Somehow, I remembered my Aunt kept chickens in a corner of the field. I climbed over the gate, and as fast as my little legs could carry me, I ran down this very steep field. There were the chickens in the hut. So, I opened the gate from the field, and then I knew I was on familiar ground. A great sigh of relief, as there was Aunt Paula's house.

I went in, and there was my Mum, Gran Stevenson, and Aunt Paula. 'Where have you been?' (I thought what a silly question!). 'Looking for Aunt Paula's house,' I replied. Mum said, 'Why?' So, I told Mum all about Gran Stevenson and the chitterlings. I could see my Mum was very angry with Gran and she turned on her. 'You know I told you not to give Faith greasy food; she can't eat it, as it makes her ill. I will not let you have my daughter again'. Aunt Paula gave me something to eat. 'You must be starved, my love,' Aunt Paula said.

Mum took me back on the bus to Teignmouth. Going home on the bus I told Mum about Grandad. 'What did Gran mean he was blind?' Mum replied, 'He can't see.' This really confused me. He had eyes, didn't he? 'But Mum, he shaved himself with something like a knife (open razor) not like Uncle Ted and Dad use a razor?' Mum said, 'He goes by touch, he feels.' But this still didn't make sense to me, as he was standing in front of a mirror, looking at himself! Later on, I thought about it when I was older. Gran Stevenson would have put the bowl of water in the same place every day where they washed, and

Gran would done her hair in front of that mirror. Mum asked me how I found my way to Aunt Paula's, so I told her. Mum said it was nothing short of a miracle for me to find my way on my own! Again, I looked puzzled. I never felt I was on my own, I felt someone was there with me. People do say we have got a guardian angel and I know I had one that day, as I have felt many times in my life since then, as you will see as I go on.

2

I was coming up to four years old and we moved again to Parson Street and Mum had another baby, a sister called Norma, born November 1938. She died at the age of three months. I can remember that day so clearly as my brother Colin was an awful prankster. He told me to stand by him and I would see the devil taking our baby sister Norma away. Colin said, 'Look up the stairs to Mum's bedroom,' and like a fool I did. Out of the bedroom door I saw a giant of a man come out, dressed all in black even to a top hat, and as he came down the stairs he was carrying this tiny white box on his shoulder, the coffin, I gave one almighty shriek, and fled through the passageway as if the devil himself was after me.

As I was four years old now in 1938, Mum was working to support our little family in between having babies. I was sent to the Catholic School as they took children in at four years of age. I went there for about a year. Then Colin got himself expelled, so Mum took both April and me away, and we all went to Brookhill School in 1939. I went into the baby class, Miss Pidgeon's, as I was only five. I loved it there as most of the children I knew went to that school, and I was far happier there. In the afternoon we had to lay on rush mats for a nap. Colin was still up to his usual tricks and told me one day that if I told lies, God would put a black mark in 'His little black book', and I would have to pay for it 'later'. So, until this day, I may tell a little white lie not to hurt someone's feelings, and I still think 'there goes another black mark, as a lie is a lie. But it is not in my nature to hurt people, so I hope God will forgive me.'

As I said before, Dad was always popping in and out of our lives and along came another sister in November 1939. Peggy Ann was born in Parson Street. I was five years and nine days older than her. She was not a happy baby. She never seemed to smile very much and was always so serious. Dad, in 1939, enlisted back into the army.

In late 1939 we moved to Higher Brook Street and Mum had another son in 1940. He only lived for a few minutes. I was still only in my fifth year. This was when things completely changed for me, and my childhood was gone over night and a lot more responsibility was put on my shoulders. I had to help clean the house, because Mum had to work to support us as much as 16 hours a day and at that tender age I realised she needed my help. I was so willing to learn how to do things for Mum, but she could be a hard taskmaster.

If she was on a late shift Mum needed my help. She taught me how to bath my baby sister. She had marked the bath for how much water I needed to put in, so I wouldn't drown her, and how to test the water to see how hot it was, by testing it with your elbow in it. I also learnt to put her nappy on; not the new ones of today, but the terry towelling ones you had to put this big safety pin in! Then I would dress her ready for bed, then feed her with the bottle. One of Colin's chores was to make the bottle and I would feed her after testing the milk on the back of my hand. This didn't happen very often, thank goodness, because if I didn't do things right, I would get a smack. Peggy would never believe me. She would say Colin had done it; Colin had bathed her because he was three years older than me. But she didn't know Mum very well, and how Victorian she was. No way would Mum let Colin touch his bare baby sister's body! But it was Mum who always liked to wind her herself and to put Peggy to bed.

One day in early 1940, still only five, as I wouldn't be six until November, I had to take Peggy to Gran Richards, my Dad's Mum. She lived at 4 Myrtle Hill. I had to wash Peggy and dress her, strap her in the pram and put the hood up. I followed Mum's instructions to the letter. When I look back on it, I wonder how I did it all at such a tender age. The pram was a big heavy wooden boat shape, what they called a high pram where you could sit two older children in, facing each other, by taking out the middle bit so they could sit daggling their legs down. I must have been about five and a half, maybe a bit more. I know Peggy was sitting up by this time, but I could only just reach the handlebar of this pram. I pushed this heavy boat shape pram up the incline towards Brookhill School.

I got to the top thinking it would be easier going down the hill. My mistake! Anyone living in Teignmouth before the war would know how steep the hill was to Lower Brook Street and the railway station. The pram picked up momentum and was going faster and faster down the hill. I was hanging on like grim death. The pram was pulling me along scrapping my legs which were bleeding and full of gravel, until I couldn't hang on anymore. The pram ended up upside down at the bottom of the hill. Luckily for me Peggy was strapped in and the hood was up, so she wasn't hurt, just frightened and screaming her head off. Some kind people stood the pram up again, so I went on my way. No one noticed my poor legs, all I got was 'Poor baby, she was frightened.'

No one asked if I was alright. I remember I was shaking like a leaf, but I said thankyou to the nice people, for helping me. I got to my Gran's and she bathed and cleaned my legs and dressed them. By this time Peggy had stopped crying. Gran said she was alright, gave me a big hug and kiss, and off I went to school. When I got home from school Mum gave me a good thrashing and called me a stupid girl. I ran out of the house crying, down to my Gran Richards's and told her what had happened. She gave me a kiss and cuddle to calm me down.

Gran was the only one who ever gave me a cuddle and a kiss that I can remember, other than my Dad when he took that boil out of my knee, but I must be fair, I think Mum never had the time as she worked long hours. Gran put her hat and coat on and took me home. But didn't Gran go for my Mum! 'The pram is much too heavy for Faith to bring down that steep hill. She is not much more than a baby herself; she can hardly reach the handlebars. In future, if you want me to look after Peggy you must bring the pram to the bottom of the hill yourself and then Faith can bring the pram the rest of the way.'

Gran was my salvation, she dressed my legs until they were better, and I would often stay with her for a few days at a time. As a treat she would take me to the pictures. Colin and April said I was Gran's favourite, but I don't think so. She loved us all, I think. Looking back on it, it was to give me a break from all the hard work I had to do. But I must say this, Mum did keep us together as a family and for this we must feel very grateful, even if Colin and I had to work so very hard. We didn't mind the hard work, but we didn't like the smacks alongside the ear, which Colin and I thought that was very unfair, as we did try so hard to please Mum.

3

Life carried on much the same for us, until Sunday 7th July 1940 when I was five years and eight months old. It had been a very lovely sunny day and Mum didn't have to go work that evening, so after tea she took all five of us for a walk along the seafront where there were a lot of people strolling along the promenade. It was just before seven o'clock. We had just passed the pier, going toward the nearest sunken garden, which is not there now, and a small aeroplane came so low over the pier that you couldn't see any markings on the plane. Most of us started to wave to the pilot. I could see him quite plainly. He had a flying helmet on his head which was fawn/sandy colour and his tunic was the same colour. He waved with his right hand, then he dropped his arm down in the cockpit; the bomb dropped with a thud and then came the bomb blast, shooting water, sand and other rubble, high into the air from the seabed. There came the sound of breaking glass and then the screaming started.

Mum told me to sit down with my back toward the sunken garden wall with April and Theo either side of me. She put Peggy on my lap and positioned this big boat shaped pram in front of us and told us to sit there until she came back. Mum went back to look for Colin as he had slipped onto the pier as we passed it. There were several people with injuries from the blast of the bomb and flying glass, and we heard one young lady died of her wounds later, but we didn't know how badly the other people were hurt. Mum found Colin alright and we went home. A sad ending to what should have been a lovely evening out with my Mum.

That is when our bombing started, and when we started to sleep in the cupboard under the stairs. Later, we were issued with a Morrison shelter, which was put under the stairs. I remember it was very frightening to hear the bombs exploding all around. The house shook, as our back yard overlooked the railway lines and was not far from the station. We just clung to each other wondering if it would be our house next with Mum every now and then saying, 'That was close.'

But the next day everything went on the same. Colin had his chores peeling the veg every day, and dicing it up, cleaning all the shoes and keeping the yard tidy and there may have been other things I can't think of now. My chores were to make the beds and to clean out the grate. This had to be done every day. Colin and I would share some of these chores and April would help with the dishes sometimes.

Every Saturday I would have to scrub out every room in the house, from top to bottom and polish any room that had lino on it. On a wet day it was hard to get a shine on the floor. If it was not to Mum's liking, I would have a slap from Mum and made to do it all over again. Our home was always spotless as you can see. I can still picture Colin and April with rags on the bottom of their feet trying to help me polish on a wet day. They were a lovely brother and sister, but I still had to look after Theo and Peggy as well.

I would have only been between six or seven years old then. One time, when I was staying with my Gran Richards, we were coming home from the pictures at about five o'clock in the afternoon on 13th August 1942. My Gran's daughter, my Aunt Winnie, lived at the end of Hollands Road, (the house is not there anymore). She asked Gran in for a cup of tea. So, in we went, and I played with my two cousins, Vincent and Chrissie. The air raid siren went off. Another air raid. We all got under the big table. After the raid Gran and Aunt Winnie, said 'That was a near thing,' and it was. It was just up the road, across from the Railway Station. It was number five Myrtle Hill that had a direct hit, and Gran's cottage which was number four and Uncle Victor's number six were all demolished by the same bomb. If we had been in the cottage, we might have been killed like Uncle Ted's dog was, as it was in the cottage at that time. That was a very near thing for Gran and me. I might not have been here writing my memoirs if it hadn't been for Aunt Winnie. Gran went to live with one of her other daughters, Aunt Barbara.

4

I will resume my memoirs with the next air raid, that was also very close for our family. I don't remember why we were not at school that day. Most likely we had caught something contagious, and we were not allowed back until it cleared. So, we were having the time of our life, playing on the defence bars on the beach (where we shouldn't have been!) We had forgotten all about the time until one of us looked at St. Michael's church clock and realised we would be late home.

We started to hurry back for home. When we got to Bickford Lane, Colin said, 'You'd better run on Faith, and make a start on things before Mum comes home, or you and I will be in for a good slap across the ear. I will bring on the little ones.' Off I went. It would have been just before four o'clock in the afternoon on September 2nd, 1942. I was level with the big green back door of the school. I don't remember the siren going off. All I can remember was hearing the awful drone of the engines of the plane, as I had heard so many times before. Looking up and seeing the big black plane, I ran on a bit faster, then I remembered that, if we were out and there was a raid, we had to run to the nearest house, so I stopped and looked back. A lady had just opened her door and called me back. A few more steps and I would have been in the thick of it, as that is the day they bombed Higher Brook Street, and Brook Hill School was blitzed. I ran back to the lady and told her my brother was coming up the hill with the little ones, so this kind lady ran down the lane. She took Peggy from Colin's arms, grabbed hold of Theo's hand, Colin took the other hand, and his little feet never hardly touch the ground. April tagged along just behind. We all tumbled under the table.

The little cottage shook. We were all frightened as we all clung to each other. Even the lady was clinging to us, as the bombing was so near. I shall never forget that lady. Every time I pass the cottage now, I think of her, she was so kind. I think we could have owed her our lives that day! After the all clear this lady said, 'All of you wait here, I will see if I can find your Mother.' In a few minutes she was back again. She told us she would have to go the long way around as the

Police had cordoned off the top of Bickford Lane. So, we stayed in her cottage until she came back with Mum.

I was seven years and nine months and I still can't believe what happened next. Maybe, this lovely lady who saved our lives that day might have been worried about her own children who were at school, but she had put us first, and then had to witness what my Mum said and did that day. We ran out to Mum, only for us three older children to get a smack alongside of the ear, and to be told, 'Fancy going into that dirty woman's house with all the nits!' I thought how nasty it was of my Mum! After all what that lady had done for us. I felt so ashamed of my Mum. I know my Mum collapsed shortly after that, but I don't know when, as we were all in a state of shock ourselves. All I can remember was we were taken to Newton Abbot for a week with our Aunt Paula.

As that was the day we lost our home in the Blitz, all we had was the clothes we stood up in. But Miss Best my teacher lost her Mum and her sister in that raid, as they only lived across the street from us. I often feel sorry for that lovely lady that cared so much for us. I hope she forgave Mum for what she said, as we were told later that Mum had also been in a state of shock. Where the police had cordoned off Higher Brook Street and Fore Street, my Mum was franticly clawing and screaming at the policeman, 'My children are under that rubble!'

They said if she could have got past the Policeman, she would have dug us out with her bare hands. Mum never showed very much feeling towards us three older children. I can only remember her hugging and kissing the two younger ones. From when I was about three years, I don't ever remember mum hugging and kissing us three older children. We were never jealous of the young ones, because we had this loving bond between the three of us that built up over the years. We looked out for each other and cared even in our adulthood. But I hope my mum in her heart did love us. I was one of those children that grew up before my years. My Gran Richards taught me how to love, she was so gentle, so sweet. I still feel for my mum, as I did love her. Going back again, mum ended up in hospital with T.B. and a nervous breakdown.

5

Gran Richards and Aunt Barbara took us up to North Wales to a little place called Four Crosses, near Llanymynech not far from Oswestry, in late September 1942. The train stopped at a wooden platform in the middle of the road, or that is what it looked to me anyway. This was where my Gran Richards's eldest daughter lived, Aunt Yvonne. She was lovely, hugs all the way round. Neomi Richards and May Jean, two of our cousins, came with us from Teignmouth, but they didn't stay long. We stayed for about eighteen months, loving every moment of it.

Aunt Yvonne found us a lovely little cottage next to the church, but we didn't stay there long. In early 1943 we moved to another cottage about three miles from the village, so we had to walk three miles to school every day. That was when Neomi and May went back to Teignmouth. The school was only one big classroom. We were all in the one class with one teacher. I didn't learn anything there, they were far too advanced with their English, and I didn't know what the teacher was talking about half the time.

I was just starting double writing at home, but I could have done the Maths standing on my head. We were more advanced with our Maths. It would have been better for me to move down a grade for English and up a grade for Maths. We loved it in the new cottage, and we didn't mind the three-mile walk both ways, as we didn't have to do any housework now or look after the two young ones. Mostly the walk was across fields, then we had to go over a style, on to a little lane, then over a canal bridge down the main road to school. It was a lovely walk when it wasn't raining.

Colin and I got a job on the nearby farm working weekends and holidays. They welcomed us with open arms as they were shorthanded with the men away at war. They couldn't get over how hard we worked as youngsters, getting in the harvest and other work around the farm. We were paid in food, eggs, butter, cheese, milk, chicken and other meats sometimes. Gran and Aunt Barbara were pleased with us. We ate well and never went hungry while we were there plus … if we worked all day on the farm, we got meals as well. We were happy and carefree. It was lovely there, loved by the people and with no bombs dropping around us. It was idyllic and there were no slaps across the head and no looking after the little ones.

We made friends there. One Saturday I took Theo with me to the farm. I thought he might like it as I only needed to collect eggs around the farm that day. All the fowl were free range and you didn't know where you would find the eggs. It took a long time to look into every crook and cranny. Theo was enjoying himself. With all the little chicks and ducklings around him he thought it was lovely being around the farm with me. He thought it was fun, until the geese spotted us and started to chase us. It was frightening with their long necks out and hissing at us. I think this was another day poor little Theo's legs never touched the ground as I pulled him along with one hand and held the basket of eggs in the other. The farmer's wife saw our plight and came out and shooed the geese away. She advised me never to run, just shoo them away and they would go.

She gave us a drink of milk and a welsh cake. 'What a lovely lot of eggs you have collected,' she said, in her lovely welsh lilt. She started to put some of the eggs in a bowl of water. 'Do you want me to wash them for you?' I asked. 'No,' she said, 'it is to see if they are good or bad, if they float they are bad or addled as we say, if they sink they are good to eat.' The Farmer's wife gave us some eggs to take home, but Theo never came on the farm again, I don't think he liked the geese.

Mum came out of hospital and then came to Wales to join us late 1943. Gran stayed with us, but Aunt Barbara went back to Teignmouth. Mum continued to let Colin and me work on the farm. We were pleased about that. It would have been silly to stop us, as the food came in handy. One day Mum asked Theo and me to fetch a pail of water from the well at the bottom of the garden. Off we went down to the well. There we saw this great big toad swimming around, we looked at each other, smiled and nodded at each other and caught the toad in the pail of water. So off we go up the garden path with big grins on our faces and took the pail of water and toad up to Mum, putting the pail gingerly on the kitchen floor. We started to run for the door, Mum gave out an almighty scream and the pail of water and toad came flying after us. My Mum shouted out, 'You little devils!' We kept laughing our heads off as we ran. It was a very happy time there.

When it was time to get the harvest in, it was totally different to today. It was cut, put into sheaves and stacked for so long to dry. Then I can't remember as I think some machinery had to do the threshing. All that was left was straw. I think this was still made into bails. Then there was the hay to get in, which was put on a wagon and made into haystacks. I might have got some of this wrong as all I can remember was using pitchforks to toss the hay up on to the waggon. They were long days in the fields, but we loved it. Colin and I were never afraid of hard work.

Some days we would go out with the school to collect rose hips and stinging nettles. This would be late summer as the stinging nettles didn't sting when they were dying off. We all had gloves on just in case. The teachers told us it was to make medicine.

Sometime after Christmas in 1944 Mum went back to Teignmouth to find us a new home, also for Gran, as you will remember we were both bombed out. For a while Gran Richards was left to look after us, but Mum was soon back with the news that she had found us new homes back at Teignmouth. We had a three bedroom-house in Chapel Street and Gran was around the corner in a two-bedroom house in Featherstone Place. Once again, Chapel Street and Featherstone Place don't stand today, as there was a new road built there instead.

February 1944 arrived, and it was now time to leave Wales. The Welsh people packed us up with blankets, sheets, pillows, cups, and plates, clothes; you name it and it was there, plus food. They were sad to see us go. They had been wonderful to us. Even the farmer and his wife took time off to say goodbye. 'What are we going to do without our little helpers now?' they said and gave Colin and me a big hug. I think I left a bit of my heart there that day. I went back when I was in my fifties. There was chap in the bar that remembered our little family. We talked for a while about the good old days, and the friends we made there. I thought how nice it was to be remembered like that after all that time.

6

I was nine years and three months old as we set foot back in Teignmouth. Things had changed here for there had been more bombing. We soon found the pea soup kitchen in Willy Lane, and Mum would send us up with a large green enamel jug from our wash hand basin which we bought back from Wales. We would pay our money and be given tokens. They were like coins, but some had bits cut off, which would tell the server lady just how much soup to give us in our jugs. The pea soup was a lovely meal for us, we all enjoyed it.

But as I said, there had been more bombing while we were away from Teignmouth. In Chapel Street there was no bridge now, so we had to go through a cutting by the railway lines into Saxe Street. Or we had to go down the hill into Chapel Street past the bombed buildings and into Teign Street. This all became a part of our playground. I went back to school. At this time, I can't remember which teacher I was with, Miss Short or Miss Price. I might have been in both classes, I don't know!

Mum was working evenings now, so we all had to be in by five o'clock so that she could lock us in before she went to work. The tea was on the table, doorsteps with marg on for us three older children and dainty sandwiches with butter and sometimes jam for Peggy and Theo. Mum said they needed the extra nourishment. We cleaned up after our tea, then we went to bed, but not Colin and April, they had other plans, as Colin was about twelve, and April was ten and a few months. They worked out how to climb out through the back-bedroom window, with help from me, then off they would go, while I looked after Theo and Peggy, then helped Colin and April back through the window before Mum came home. I don't know if Mum ever cottoned on.

I don't know if we came back to find our town filled with Americans, or if they arrived after we came home, but it was no more a sleepy little town. We were overrun by Americans who had taken over all our hotels on the sea front and our Pavilion Theatre which became their mess hall. We really didn't mind much, as they gave us a lovely party for the children once. I remembered as it was the first time our little family tasted ice cream. 'Yummy, yummy!'

I never saw so much singing and dancing going on in the street sometimes, as I did in those days, with the Americans. If it wasn't Glen Miller's 'In the Mood', it was that crazy song, 'Mairzy Doats' ringing out from every open window as you passed by the hotels. We soon learnt the words, and we were singing them, besides other songs of that time we learnt from the Americans. Although we were young, we began to understand why the Americans were like they were, dancing and singing in the street. It was 'To live for today, as tomorrow you might die.' I think this was their motto as they waited for the great exodus from Britain, as we now know what happened. The great invasion was soon to take place. God bless all of them that took part in this to save us. So many didn't return home.

It makes you think! All those countries that became united and fought as one to keep the enemy at bay from our shores and freed other countries that had been defeated in Europe and Egypt. Italy was where my Dad was wounded and convalesced in Rome. When we won the war in Europe they didn't stop there, they went on to the Far East, where we had forces that had been fighting the Japanese for a long time. At long last that war ended in peace, with dancing and parties again in the street. It was the end of World War Two. We must never forget all who lost their lives for our freedom. I had to put this in here as I feel so strongly about it. I was one of the children that carried around a gasmask and went through most of the bombing. I know what it was like to sleep under the stairs in a Morrison shelter, clinging to your brother and sister as the bombs were dropping all about you. But we were the lucky ones. We are still here to tell the tale. But we should never forget and should always pay tribute on the eleventh hour of the eleventh day of the eleventh month, of every year.

I forgot to tell you about the ration books! All our food was on ration, as well as clothes and petrol and it went on for quite a while after the war, some of it even going on in to the 1950's. All I know about it was the amounts were very meagre. The amount of cheese we might eat in one sitting now had to last the whole family for a week, but it didn't make any difference to us. Our food had always been very meagre.

We settled into Chapel Street in February 1943. I was nine and three months and started back at school. I soon caught up with my maths as this was my best subject, my English and spelling speaks for itself, still very childlike, but with a dictionary and plenty of common sense that has got me through life.

We soon made friends with the children in Saxe Street, running down Sun Lane to go for a swim at high tide on the quay, in our swim suits, no shoes, and no towel, for if we had, they might have been pinched, as things were still in short supply. When I first came back to Teignmouth when I was in my ninth year I couldn't swim to speak of, maybe one or two strokes and I would go under. This day I was sat on the wall at the end of the quay, now in my tenth year, talking with the other children, when this boy pushed me in the water at high tide thinking I was April. There was April up the top, screaming her head off, 'Faith can't swim!' From that day on, Faith *did* swim, and my swimming got stronger and stronger. By the way, the boy that pushed me in the water was Tim Johnson who later became my Brother-in-law when he married Peggy. Tim and I often had a good laugh about it.

When we came back to Teignmouth it was as if we had never left. Mum was back to her old ways hitting Colin and me if we didn't get things right, having to do all the housework and I now had to look after Peggy and Theo again, and they were a right handful. Now Peggy would have been about five, and Theo would have been eight years and a few months, and they would do anything to get me into trouble. I am sure they would do this just to see Mum hitting me, because I would cry, and they would laugh. Colin and April would stick up for me, but to no avail, as Mum would give me and Colin and April another slap. Then Mum would say, 'It is your place, Faith, to keep them in order.' Mum would never chastise Theo and Peggy at all. Mum would just say, 'Little ones don't tell lies, it is only you, older ones that are liars.'

My Colin got fed up with this. 'It is not fair, we do our best to please Mum, and those little brats are always getting you into trouble Faith. It's not fair! You leave it to me, and get on with your work Faith, I'll sort them out!' Colin had had an idea, he stepped in to help me. Colin threatened them and told them he would lock them in a dark cupboard with the spiders for a day, if they didn't do what Faith told them to do. There was never any more nonsense from them. It did the trick. Thank goodness!

In early 1945, still about ten years and a half, as my birthday was not until November, still the baby of the class, we had to take the first part of our eleven plus, as a lot of the children were eleven in this class by now. Before I took the second half of the test, which the other children took while I was in hospital, I became ill. I came home from school one day feeling very poorly and asked Mum if I could go right to bed. 'Sit down and eat your tea,' she said. I took one look at the doorstep made of bread and marg, 'but Mum I can't even swallow water!' This is when my April chipped in. 'Mum, she must be poorly, she didn't eat her figgy duff at school today, she gave it to me.' But that didn't stop my Mum from giving me a good thrashing. 'Look at your lovely colour! Get out of my sight! You make sick,' she said crossly.

When I woke up, I was in hospital. How long I had been in the state of delirium, I didn't know. A nurse come in and announced that I was awake, at last. The nurse told me I had scarlet fever. How long I had been asleep or drugged I don't know. I was told I was there for six weeks but to be honest it didn't seem very long. I must have been very poorly when I came into hospital. My dear Gran Richards managed to creep in around the back to see me, as the nurse said she was not allowed in, God bless her. Dad sent me a letter, to say he was convalescing in Rome, as he had been wounded in the war, and told me he was hoping to be sent home soon. 'When we are both well and out of hospital it will be lovely to see you all once again, as I am missing all of you.' The letter was funny, it was like a photo on a bakealite strip not on paper. It was very small and the print was condensed. Older people could tell me more about it, I expect.

I was taken home by car from Torbay Isolation Hospital after six weeks. When I got indoors, Mum said, 'Are you home already! Get out and play with the others.' No hugs and kisses. No 'nice to see you.' That was the only greeting I had. I sat on the doorstep and cried. I wasn't even eleven then, and I felt my Mum didn't love me. Along came April and Colin. They made up for it, as soon they saw me, they were all over me hugging and kissing me. 'Lovely to see you home again, Faith! We missed you.' I felt loved again. God bless them.

Shortly after that, the school sent Mum a letter saying that I had missed the second half of my eleven plus but since I had passed the first half, I would still be allowed to sit for the second half. If I had passed the first half with my maths, I don't think I would have passed the second half.

At this moment it is 2019, and my daughter Lydia is up for the weekend and we were talking over old times and I came out with, that I remembered going to the Grammar School to take an English exam. This could have been my eleven plus. It was a multiple-choice of three words 'there,' 'their,' and I can't remember what the third word was. We had to put the correct word in the sentence, and that is all I could remember. Lydia said I should put it in my story. I still don't know one way or the other. I walked into the room where Mum and Gran Richards were having a disagreement about it. 'There is no need for her to take the exam, as no girl of mine is going to Grammar School!' As I said before, Mum was very Victorian, and didn't believe in girls being educated.

Dad came home from the war in January 1946. I was eleven and two months. He came home with five awards and medals, the 1939-45-Star, the Africa Star, Italy Star, War medal 1939 -1945, and Defence Medal. It was lovely having him home. He seemed to spend a lot of time with us children, showing us how to draw and colour; he was a good artist. He showed us some of the drawings he did in Rome. But he would also love to sing and would sing with us. His favourite song was 'Red Sails in The Sunset'. We soon learnt the words. But alas it didn't last long, as dad and mum had a blazing row. Dad packed his bag and left for good. We children were very sad to see him go. He had only been home for a short while and we had enjoyed having him home with us, as things were so much better for us.

In January 1946 I started Westlawn School. I loved it there. We also went to Torquay indoor swimming baths to start training for our swimming exams with the school. I started receiving my certificates, as I soon became a strong swimmer. I did about three or four different strokes and I had a certificate for each one, so I put them up on the bedroom wall. One day I came home from school and there on the bed were all my certificates ripped up in tiny pieces. Peggy and Theo had a smirk on their faces looking quite pleased with themselves. I was mad. I could have hit them, but I didn't. I went to Mum about it, which was an utter waste time, as Mum said, 'Why are you making so much fuss about it? It's only bits of paper!' But to me it was far more than that, it was proof that I had accomplished something in my life. With Peggy being over seven and Theo over ten at the time, I think Mum should have chastised them. But Mum's little dears could do nothing wrong.

As Colin, April, and I became old enough, we had to do paper rounds before going to school, as well as our work at home. Mum took all the money we earned. Peggy was never expected to do anything, but I was surprised to see Theo do a bread round when he came of age. We thought he was able to keep some of his money but were never sure.

There is one thing I forgot to mention about when we lived in Higher Brook Street. I would stay up late to help Mum with the mending some evenings. She taught me how to knit, sew and to do needlework. From those early days until I left home Mum showed me a lot how to read patterns and to do the different knitting and sewing stitches. But most of all, she was a lot softer at these times. Mum told me about Dad and my very early childhood which is why I am able to write about it.

Mum talked about her childhood, about how her brother, my Uncle Walter on my Mum's side of the family, had taught her how to read and write before he went away to the war and was killed in the First World War, when she was about four. Mum went on to tell me how Grandad enlisted again in the army to try and get out to France to see his son's grave. But he was too old to be sent to France, so he told the army how old he was and went back to the farm. Mum said she would have loved to go out to France, but the chance never arose. Last year, in 2018, myself, my daughter Rosie, and my grand-daughter Zoe and husband were able to fulfil that dream and lay a wreath at his memorial with great pride and tears. This was one of the times I asked Mum about April, 'Why doesn't April do any work around the house?' Mum answered by saying that she was not reliable. I still didn't understand what she meant. Now and again April had to do the dishes and that was all, Mum said.

I think this little story that Mum told me is why I loved my Mum. On one of the evenings, she was telling me of her stay in hospital. She had rheumatic fever and became very worried about us children having a roof overhead and enough food. Gran Richards was looking after us, so the only thing Mum could do was to apply to the means test people while she was in hospital. She told me what these people had said. It is so hard to believe what they said and how cruel things were back in those days.

They told my Mum, 'You must put the children in a home, and when you are well enough you can go back into service!' Mum immediately signed herself out of hospital and found work just to keep the family together. I shall always love her for it. I don't know when this happened.

Thinking about this now, when *did* it happen. And how many of us children were born at the time? I would have put it roughly before or shortly after Theo was born when we lived in Clampet Lane, because of my memory, and this would have been the only time I couldn't remember until we lived in Willow Street. That was 1937 when I was coming up to three years old. So, it would have been somewhere between 1935 to 1937. The only time I remembered mum was missing, was in the war, and she had T.B and a nervous breakdown when we went to Wales in 1942, and Gran did look after us then. I would have remembered if Gran was with us in Willow Street.

I can tell from my Dad's army records, which I have, that he was up in Haslemere with Mum and Colin and still in the Army until 6th October 1932. They must have stayed in Haslemere as I know April was born in Haslemere in April 1933. Gran wouldn't have been up in Haslemere with them then, as she never left Devon until she went to Wales. So, I was born in 1934. Mum was back in Teignmouth, but she said she had no one to look after her and the children. But why didn't Gran look after us? Did they fall out? I think Gran said she looked after Theo, so the only time it could have been is when Mum lived in Clampet Lane and she was ill with rheumatic fever. I found out just today, on the 13th April 2020, while turning out things and finding my birth certificate, that both Mum and Dad were living with Gran Richards at Myrtle Hill when they came back from Haslemere. This would make a lot of sense and Gran would have been looking after us before we moved to Clampet Lane.

Now I am writing this I wonder if Mum's memory was very clear about everything. Paul, my son, and I tried to find out when the workhouse closed down but found nothing. Again, this afternoon 8th April 2019, I tried. I was born in 62 East Street, Newton Abbot in the grounds where the workhouse stood. That is all I can find out. Whether it was the workhouse then, I don't know. Or was something said to hurt me?

I just found out today, the 9 April 2019 that it *was* in the workhouse grounds. In 1901 it had become The Public Assistance Institution for mothers who could not afford a midwife or a doctor. But as it was the name 'workhouse' that was written to me, the old name has stuck. But it was the poor house then. Sometimes my Mum would say some awful things about me like, 'You were behind the door when the looks was given out' or 'only Peggy is the pretty one of the family.' This is strange since we three youngest looked like peas in a pod. It was the same about my bust. I know it was small but what's the odds? I was very athletic, it suited me! And the other thing Mum was always on about, was my shoe size. Mum would say my shoes were the boxes hers came in! She took a size five and was about five foot two inches. I was five foot nine inches, and took a size six, not a lot in it. Mum threw this kind of thing at me all through my teens. It was not nice. Mum belittled me so much I got very withdrawn and lacked confidence. I went through life like this. People can still easily knock me now. I thought of myself as an ugly duckling with big feet.

9

The summer holiday of 1946 was when my brother Colin got into trouble with the police. A mob of boys had ransacked the Seacroft Hotel, and Colin came up before the judge. Now the Judge thought Colin and another boy had been led astray by the older boys, so the judge said all they needed was discipline, so both had to go into an apprentice school. Colin went in the army and the other boy went in the navy. When they came of age Colin ended up in Korea in 1952. Both this young man and Colin said it was the making of them, so the judge had done right by them.

This same summer holiday Theo and I now became pals, and sometimes April would come with us. We would play on the bomb buildings, or on the beach, or go for long walks up to Haldon, Bishopsteignton or along the seawall to Dawlish. We would pick wildflowers and watercress to go with our bread and marg and were sometimes lucky enough to find mushrooms. We would pick blackberries and Mum would make jam and I would help by putting the blackberries through the sieve to get the seeds out. Sometimes the farmer would leave windfall apples by his gate, and Mum would make a tart, but if she didn't have enough flour and marg she would do a custard with the apple and blackberries. This is when I started to learn to cook.

I still had to do my work before going out. As Peggy was about seven, I don't remember her wanting to come out with us, so most days she stayed home on her own. It must have been alright with Mum. But Theo loved to come with me, though April was more interested in boys now. So, Theo and I were on our own one day, and we started to walk on a sandbank. Lovely soft sands. We stopped to make a fort with a moat around it, but we were unaware that the tide was coming in around the side of us. By the time I noticed it, we were out of our depths.

I was alright, but it was Theo! He could only do doggie paddle a little. I never did my life saving, so how was I go to get him back to shore? I told Theo he had to keep going once we were in the water,

'As long as you can, we've got to swim for it. I will stay with you all the time; I won't leave you!' So off we go. Between us, I managed to keep his chin up out of the water for most of time, and with a lot of encouragement on my part, we swam. Every now again I would try to touch the bottom. Being tall for my age at last my foot touched the sandy bottom. With a sigh of relief, I was able to grab hold of Theo, who was just about on his last legs. I pulled him the rest of the way, with him just hanging on to me. I don't think he would have lasted much longer. A narrow squeak for us both. I couldn't go home without Theo. I think Mum would have killed me! But that was the day he learnt to swim. Theo was full of himself! He never told Mum what really happened, only that *I* had taught him to swim that day. It was lucky for me!

Now and again, in the evenings we would see our Uncle Ted, my Dad's brother, who lived with his mother, my Gran Richards. He would be fishing by rowing a boat out in a semicircle, putting nets out in the water as he went, then people on both sides would pull the net in. We loved to help as we pulled the net in, all the fish were in the back of the net and we then had to sort them as the small ones had to be thrown back in the sea again. After the fish were sorted Uncle Ted would give us some to take home to Mum. We loved fish and I still do.

Uncle Ted was like a father to me. At every opportunity I would be with Gran Richards. I loved her. She was so kind and gentle and taught me how to appreciate so much, like the sunset going down over Shaldon Bridge, and lots of other things too numerous to mention. I think this was the making of who I am today. 'Thank you, Gran!' In the winter I would go down to the Jug and Bottle to get her stout; something called half and half. I would have a sip of it on the way home to Gran's. When I got back Gran would put a red-hot poker in the jug of stout. She would be knitting a seaman jumper for Uncle Ted with thick wool, but was finding it very hard now as she had arthritis in her hands so would hold her long needle under her armpit and hold it with her arm and could do the plain row with ease, but when I was there she would get me to knit the purl row back, as she found this very hard.

Like Mum, Gran would tell all about her side of the family; who we were related to and how, which cousin was which and what family they belonged to. So, between mum and Gran I had a lot of knowledge of both sides of the family, so later on in life it was not hard to piece the family together and to make the family tree. Paul, my son, started to take an interest in it so we went up to Exeter and found out a lot more. We took Gran's side back to 1552. It was hard work as we found out there were twelve different ways of spelling Gran's maiden name, but my Paul was often picking my brains to find out more, which he did.

10

It was 1947. The summer was over. Back to school! I went back to school in April's old clothes, including her shoes which were a size too small. Now April was short, a bit on the plump side, I was much taller than her, so her clothes just about came down and covered my bottom. The fashion was about an inch below the knee at that time. I was happy until this day at Westlawn School. I was coming up to my thirteenth birthday when the bullying started. 'You are a freak,' they would say. They would chant, 'We can see your knickers!' I was a very shy and timid girl. This gang of girls would hit and kick me all because of the way I was dressed, and how tall I was. I had shot up and I was taller than all the children and most of the teachers too.

I was this tall stick-like person with no shape at all and was nothing but a laughingstock. Dressed in April's clothes, I looked even taller. But one day the bullying went too far. I couldn't take it anymore. I was so upset, that I ran to my Gran's house. I told her what had been happening at school. Gran gave me a hug and a kiss. On went her hat and coat and off we went to Mum's. There was a big row, but my Mum could not be moved. Mum said that the new clothes had to go to the eldest child, not the youngest. Gran said to Mum, 'is this your last word on it?' Mum said 'Yes, Faith will just have to take what the girls hand out.' Gran said, 'So, you don't care if Faith is being a laughingstock and bullied?' Mum didn't answer Gran. But Gran said, 'I will not see any of my grandchildren being treated this way!'

Gran went on to say, 'Well, from now on I will buy Faith two gymslips, an overcoat and shoes for the winter and two dresses and sandals for the summer. By the way I shall be up this Saturday to take Faith to buy her gymslips and shoes.' On the twentieth of November, Gran took me to buy my new overcoat for my thirteenth birthday. I can't say I remembered the name of the shop now, but it was in Fore Street just up from the London Hotel, past Campet Lane next to Hayes the Butchers. The ground floor was a haberdashery and upstairs they sold clothes. Gran and I went upstairs only to see the shopkeeper and salesgirls sitting around this box that was showing pictures. It was called a T.V. I had never seen one before! They got a chair for Gran, and I sat on the floor bedside her and you can't guess what we were watching; it was the Queen and Prince Philip's wedding. I thought I was the luckiest girl to have such a day to remember, the twentieth November 1947. I don't think I will ever forget that day, and with a smart new navy-blue coat as well!

After that things settled down and I was happy again at school. For the next year everything was much the same, do paper round in the morning before going school and cleaning the house. I had learnt how to cook by now and did some of the cooking at home. I was always allowed out to play, even for a while in the evening sometimes, so long as the work was done first. I didn't have to look after Theo and Peggy, but Theo would come out with me most of the time. In the warmer weather we would swim a lot or make dens on the bomb sites and play cowboys and indians. I was a proper tomboy at this time but that was all whilst I was growing up.

In 1947 Theo started Grammar School. April left school at the age of fourteen and went to work at the Maudrift. It was a live-in job; I only saw her on her days off. On pay days Mum was always outside of the Maudrift and she would take most of April's money, which I don't think she was entitled to, as April did not live at home then. That was when she started courting Nigel, after that I didn't see a lot of her. I missed her a lot.

It was the summer holidays again and I spent as much time as I could at Gran's. She took me to the pictures and sometimes to this club where I learnt some of the old-time dances in the afternoons. It was at the end of Sun Lane and Stanley Street. It was called The Athenaeum Teignmouth Unionist Club. It was now 1948 and I was coming up to fourteen. I did some jobs in the hotels like washing up, but I didn't see much of the money. Sometimes I went out with Theo as he was coming on the quay. We both loved to swim at high tide.

After the summer holidays, I went back to school. I was so happy to be back at school. I wouldn't say I was popular but well-liked by a lot of the children. They would come to me for help with their maths which they didn't understand, even some of the girls that had bullied me, but mostly it was the boys who needed maths to get good jobs, so I helped them a lot.

I loved netball and the girls would like me on their side, I think because of my height, and I loved P.E. I was good at most subjects. It was my English and spelling which I was not good at. That let me down badly. There again, the reason I didn't catch up was because, if any of the family over the years fell ill, it was me that had to stay home and look after them, so I missed a lot of schooling. But I got by with a dictionary at my side and the willingness to learn and a great deal of common sense.

11

I was going into my last year at school in 1949, this was the year my Mum remarried, but I still had to do my paper-round every morning. I also still had to do most of the housework around the home, with no offer of help from the younger two. Theo would have been twelve, and Peggy would have been nine and I had been doing the housework since I was five. This was the year mum was very ill and taken to hospital with pleurisy. While she was in hospital she lost her eyesight, but before she came out of hospital, she got the sight back in one eye. The school-board man came around once because I had been home for a while. Mum said to him, 'If you can find someone to take Faith's place, she can go back to school.' As he walked away, he shrugged his shoulders. Mum was on the mend now, soon learnt to live with the sight in one eye, and back to work she went.

I went back to school once more. The summer holidays were coming up again, that was a laugh, as there was no rest for the wicked. Bedsides cleaning the home, I still had to do my early morning paper-round for which I was paid five shillings a week. I came home, had breakfast, washed the dishes, tidied things up a bit, and on to the next job, which was working on the beach huts from ten in the morning until six o'clock in the evening. I was making sandwiches, collecting trays off the beach, washing up the dishes and serving pots of tea and snacks. We girls were kept very busy, but we did have a short break for lunch, and were given a snack and a drink. I got paid two pounds a week for that. Then off I had to go to the hotel where Mum worked, to wash the evening dishes. I had a lovely evening meal there. That was all I got, as I never saw my wages for that job. They paid Mum.

My Mum took the whole of my wages; two pounds five shillings a week, which was a lot of money in those days, plus whatever I got at the hotel. I never saw a penny of it. The only food I had at home that holiday was my breakfast, which was meagre. I wonder now how much Mum was getting in that holiday. She had wages from my stepfather! Her own wages! And she was still taking money from April! Plus, she had an allowance from Colin's and Theo's army pay! As well as all of mine! Some of this I can understand, after all the insecurity Mum must have gone through when we were younger. Mum continued to work up until the day she died at the age of 67 years and eleven months.

I went back to school for the last term. I was to be taught by the teacher who had not been very nice to me once when I was in the second year of Westlawn. Our maths teacher was away, and this teacher stood in and I just froze at the thought of a term with her! I was sitting next to my friend. Next, I was being accused of cheating. I had made some silly mistakes and run out of time to correct them, and my friend had made the same mistakes as I did. I was the one who was accused of cheating. Most of the children had their hands up. 'Please Miss, it is not Faith. She is the one that helps us all with our maths when we get stuck!' This teacher would not have it.

My friend got moved to the back of the classroom, 'and the CHEAT can stay at the front,' she said to me, 'so I can keep an eye on her,' and she gave us four more sums each. I soon finished mine and had plenty of time to double check them. I knew they were right this time. The teacher dismissed the class without apologising to me. But what happened then to my friend in the playground, I just didn't go along with. The other children sent her to Coventry, and she stayed away from school for a few days. This was all unfortunate, for the teacher had set the maths a little higher than usual and the children were not up to this standard and got most of them wrong. Even I got some of them wrong the first time.

As things turned out, my fears about the teacher were unfounded. She turned out to be so helpful. 'I see you are having some difficulty with your spelling, Faith?' I said, 'Yes, Miss. Do you know why?' So, I told her what happened when I was in Wales, also about being kept home from school when anyone in the family was ill and how I had to look after them and ended up missing out a lot. She said, 'How unfortunate for you to have missed so much schooling.' 'Yes, Miss.' 'As there are only a handful of you, may I call you young adults? I will help you all where needed.' She was a great help with my spelling and grammar, but sadly there was not enough time. I needed at least a year or more, I was so far behind. But she did her best with us and we loved her for it. She was a good teacher.

April came home at the end of 1949. Unfortunately, she was pregnant with Nigel's child, but he wouldn't marry her. April was heartbroken as she loved him very much. She had been going steady with him for a long time. Now, someone who had loved April from afar, Bert, went to my Mum and asked if he could marry April. So, April was threatened by Mum that if she didn't marry Bert she would be put in a wayward home for girls. I think they were still around at that time. Not sure. Don't forget, we came from the dark ages.

April did marry Bert and had a baby boy late December 1949. Although April resented Bert at first, he turned out to be a very good husband and father to her son and he worshipped the ground she walked on, but I don't think the feeling was mutual at the time. I did a lot of babysitting while they lived in Chapel Street in one room. I loved my little baby nephew. He was lovely.

12

I left school that December 1949, at the age of fifteen. I was offered an apprenticeship from one of my teachers as a book keeper, as he had been giving some of us girls extra lessons in typing and shorthand. The wages would start at five shillings a week! Going up yearly! But Mum had other ideas. 'Work for five shillings a week! You will go and work in the laundry and get thirty shillings a week there. And I will have a pound of that, and you can have the ten shillings. You will have to buy your personal things like your soap and toothpaste and clothes, and you will still have to clean the house from top to bottom every Saturday, unless you get overtime on Saturday, and what you earn I will have half of your overtime money.' I have just found out from Theo, my brother, (yesterday May 30th 2019) that he was the one that had to do the housework when I was doing overtime and he said Peggy didn't help, he had to do it all on his own, bedside his paper-round and his bread-round, and Mum took all his money as well!

On the first of January 1950, I started to work in the laundry. I was very much afraid of the big machinery, as it was hissing out steam and it was so noisy there that I wanted to hide in a quiet corner, but instead I was put at the back of this hissing machine, to fold pillowcases there. There was a lady putting damp pillowcases in one end of this machine, coming out from the giant rollers the other end dry. It was my place to fold them. The work was easy enough, just boring as you were standing all day and your legs began to ache, but I soon got used to it. They were a lovely lot of ladies all willing to help each other. We sang all day which kept our morale up, we learnt all the latest songs off the wireless, we would do our folding in time to the beat, we got through a lot of work and our boss was very pleased with us. 'Keep it up girls,' he would say. He was a good boss. After working eight hours a day I came home and had tea and there were still all the dirty dishes left for me to wash and there was Mum, my stepfather, Peggy and Theo sat down playing games. I just felt like the servant, instead of one of the family. I just went up to my bedroom and cried.

Shortly after starting work, I began getting fainting fits. Miss Goff the manageress, would send me home, saying I was not fit for work, and Mum would send me right back to work, saying there was nothing wrong with me. This went on for a while. Miss Goff would send me home, and Mum would send me right back. The next time I fainted one of the ladies took me home and told my Mum, 'If you don't take your daughter to the doctors, I will.'

At last Mum took me to the doctor. I don't think she would have if she wasn't shamed into it, from what happened next. The doctor said to Mum, 'You have got a very sick young lady here, she has got acute anaemia, she needs to go on to iron medicine right away, and most likely will be on it for a very long time and I would like you to bring her back from time to time.'

As we were about to leave the doctor's surgery, Mum turned around and said to the doctor, 'It's not Faith that's ill, it's Peggy!' The doctor stood up nearly knocking his chair over. 'Mrs Williams, there is nothing wrong with your Peggy, it's your Faith needs looking after.' Mum said, 'Why is Peggy so much paler than the rest of the children?' 'Most likely,' he said, 'because Peggy's corpuscles are set deeper than your other children, and theirs are closer to the surface. If you keep this up Mrs Williams, you are going to turn your Peggy into a hypochondriac.' ('*Well, that was a good prediction! You should have put some money on it!!' - this was put in by my daughter, Rosie!*) Mum sent me right back to work, but when I got home that evening and had chance, I looked up the words, hypochondriac, and corpuscles, in my dictionary. I was on iron medicine for about ten years. It was awful. I took it until I couldn't take another spoonful.

13

We were still in 1950. Bert got a new job at Powderham Estate with a tied cottage, so they moved out of Chapel Street. But sadly, the scandal of April having a baby so young, rebounded on me, and I got this pack of boys following me around asking if I was like my sister? I became very frightened as it didn't matter which way I walked home I always had to pass a bomb site. My very good friend Anna would walk home with me. You must remember I was a very shy and quiet girl, who was kept down by my Mum. Then one evening Anna's dad asked her, 'Why do you need to walk home with Faith?' Anna spoke up for me and told her dad what was happening to me. He asked me if I could name any of boys, I said that I could, and Anna's dad said he would see what he could do to stop it for me. He did stop it, except for just once more. I was at the Triangle when Nigel, April's ex-boyfriend, came up to me and asked if I was like my sister (in a very loud voice) I just saw red and punched him in the face. Most people at the bus stop knew how Nigel had treated my sister and overheard what he said to me. A big cheer went up as I punched him. I never went out with any of the Teignmouth boys, I didn't like boys at this time anyway.

Anna was now working at the laundry, and we were always out together. I bought her bicycle off her, because she wanted a new model and I paid her so much a week. We had lovely times together, walking, swimming, and going to the pictures, and now cycling. As soon as I finished my work on a Saturday in the summer, we cycled to Goodrington, to swim there. Then we would cycle back to Newton Abbot, have a pasty or chips to eat and then go to the pictures. Our favourite films were Esther William's films, because of the swimming, but I had to be home by half past nine.

I wasn't going home so much now after work in the summer. Anna would bring a sandwich for me and we would go swimming in the evening and try out some of Esther's movements. We were like a couple of water babies, and we soon had an audience. As soon as we saw all these people looking over the pier at us, we would swim under the pier. The main reason for swimming by the pier was that we would stay in the water far too long and sometimes get the cramp. But some of our friends reckon we were very good to watch.

We were always singing at work. It helped the time along. The girls got fed up with this dead-end job, so they were going to enlist in the W.A.A.F. I asked Mum if I could go. 'You are not going! What! To become an officer's ground sheet!' I wondered what Mum meant by that, so I asked the girls. They just laughed at me. 'Faith, you're so green!' And they told me. 'But your Mum's got a dirty mind,' they said. I was in my sixteenth year, and still not interested in men. Why didn't she have any trust in me? The girls were soon gone and I felt lonely for a while. Sometimes, I would get on my bike and go for a ride or a swim on my own.

Then Kate came to the laundry to work and we went out together. This is when I met my first boyfriend. He was a solider called Fred, based at Denbury Camp. He was a Londoner. He told me how his long-standing girlfriend gave him up when he was called up for National Service. Soon he was being drafted to Egypt. But before he went, he asked me to be his steady, and we would talk about marriage when he came home, but he didn't expect me to stay at home every evening, he said I was too young. Now Kate's boyfriend was also going to Egypt. So, she too enlisted in W.A.A.F. I was on my own again, so I went to the shed to get my bike and it was gone. I went to Mum and asked her where my bike was. 'I sold it,' was her response. 'But it was not your bike to sell, Mum! I bought it myself!' 'Everything in this house belongs to me,' Mum said. There was just no winning with her.

Then, in February 1952, Theo enlisted in the Army Apprentice School. Also, just after that was one of the most sorrowful times of my life. This was when my Gran Richards was very ill. My Aunty Barbara wouldn't let me in to say goodbye, she said I was too young. I was gone seventeen and all I wanted was to say thank you for all the help she had given to me in the earlier part of my life. My lovely, lovely Gran, whom I loved so very much, died without me telling her how grateful I was, and without a last kiss. I was told I could go to the funeral.

I was now moved in the Laundry to the racking department. This job was where we had to sort the clothes out ready for packing. We had to read the numbers printed on each garment and put it in its pile. I was now working with a girl named Joyce, who was very unhappy at home. She was petite and about twenty, but very underdeveloped and looking more about twelve. She said, 'Do you think you could get me a boyfriend?' I looked at her, 'I will have a try.' So that coming Saturday, off we go to Newton Abbot. We went to the pictures, then to The Blackcat café which was in the bus depot. A solider came up to me, 'I would like to take you out, would you go on a date with me?' he asked. I didn't like him at all, so I said no but he wouldn't take no for an answer at all. He was very pushy, I said, 'Alright, so long as you bring a friend along with you for my friend. No friend ... no date!' as we walked away, 'Is that fair?' I asked, and he nodded.

I can't remember what day we said we would meet, but I said to Joyce, 'Don't leave me on my own with him, I can't trust him no further than I can throw him.' Anyway, he brought a mate along called Reg. He and Joyce hit it off right away, you never saw so much happiness on a person's face. Reg took Joyce to London to meet his parents and she came back engaged, which let me off the hook. Both Joyce and Reg thanked me for what I did for Joyce, 'You were a good friend. It was worth it to see you both so happy!' I said. Reg took Joyce back to London and they were married within the month.

14

I was still writing to Fred in Egypt. It was now 1951. I still went to the pictures now and again in Newton Abbot if there was not a good film at the Rivera or the Carlton. One Saturday I went up to Newton Abbot and went to the pictures. As I was walking back to the bus depot a sailor came up to me. He started to talk, 'You always seems to be on your own, would you like to come out with me?' I told him about Fred out in Egypt, and that I was going steady with him. He said, 'That's alright with me as all my mates are courting, it will only be a platonic friendship while I am based in Plymouth. I live in East Ogwell and my name is Sid, what's yours?' I told him that I lived in Teignmouth. We started to go out together. When he was home, we went Dutch with everything, then Fred came back from Egypt, so I stopped seeing Sid.

Fred and I talked about me going to London and getting married. He said, 'I must get a job first.' So, he went back to London, found a job, and phoned me every Saturday evening from a phone box, to a phone box in Teignmouth. Then, one evening he told me he had found a flat for us. I said that was lovely and asked, 'When can I come up?' 'Not until I furnish it,' was his answer. This went on for months and I felt he was playing for time, so the next week he phoned, I said, 'Would it be better if I came and helped to finish furnishing the flat, we could do it together?' 'I have just bought a dressing table this weekend,' he said, 'No, I want it perfect for you.' 'Do you!' I retorted, and I put the phone down on him. I felt he was playing for time and trying to get his old girlfriend back. He never phoned me back. I never heard from him ever again. I think I was right. That was early 1953.

I thought, 'What can I do this evening, it's a bit late? I know, I will go to Newton Abbot and see if I can meet up with some of the girls.' I missed the bus, so I walked down to the station, and caught the train. Feeling a bit low about Fred, I got off the train, and started to walk up Queen Street to the picture house and looked to see what was on. It was too late to go to the pictures, as I had to be home by nine thirty. I was about to wander up the town when I heard a voice behind me. 'I haven't seen you for a long time. How are things?' It was Sid, and he asked me to walk down to the station with him, as he had to be back early that evening as they were off on sea trials early the next morning. I had nothing better to do so I walked down with him.

Sid said, 'I have been missing you, I thought you would be up in London married to your Fred by now.' 'Me too!' 'So, you've finished with Fred?' 'Yes, he's messed me around long enough.' 'Are you going out with someone new?' he asked. 'No, I've only just finished with Fred.' Sid's train just pulled up into the station, but just before he got on it, he asked, 'Will you be my girlfriend now?' I replied 'Yes!' He gave me the first kiss I ever had from him! Sid jumped on the train, shouting, 'I should be home next weekend, I will let you know the time and place.' When we met up again, I said, 'Sid do you want us to go steady?' He nodded. 'Well I don't want you to waste my time, I've had enough of someone dangling me on a string,' was my answer.

I was still working in the laundry and I shared the bedroom with Peggy. I found out Peggy was wearing my best clothes and undies and putting it back in my drawer dirty. This day my knickers were very soiled and had been put back in the drawer. I went to Mum and showed her the knickers. Mum said, 'You can wash them!' 'But Mum they are my clothes!' 'I told you before everything in this house belongs to me, if Peggy wants to wear it, she can.' 'But Mum I bought it myself with my own money, I worked hard for this!' But Mum turned her back on me and walked away. Once again Peggy was not chastised. The next day at work John caught me crying. 'What's up Faith?' As John was like a father figure to us young girls, I told him everything. 'That's not fair,' he said, 'let me think about it, and see if I can help.' He came back to me and said, 'Bring your clothes in every Monday. I will keep them upstairs until Friday. They will be all clean by then and ready for you for the weekends.' The knickers I threw in a dustbin and bought new ones and carried them around in my bag, as I didn't like the thought of someone wearing my under garments.

I didn't see Sid a lot, only when he had leave, or his ship was in Plymouth, but we kept steady. When he was on his summer leave, I arranged for my holidays and we stayed out at Ogwell together, with his mum and dad and two younger brothers. We got engaged that holiday, August 1953. The year of our Queen Elizabeth II's, Coronation. Mum let me get married on 10 April 1954, as I was in no

47

hurry to leave home, as I needed to get a little money behind me. I was going to have Sid's money put right in the bank and I was going to carry on working at the laundry. My Aunt Barbara made my wedding dress and bought me my headdress and veil and did all my flowers for me. She was really kind to me. We got married in St Michael's Church, Teignmouth.

Mum said we could have the reception at home. I think we paid for most of that as Mum took all the money we were given for wedding presents to pay for the reception. We went to Torquay for our honeymoon and spent the last week at Ogwell where the in-laws gave us a room of our own. I started to stay at the in-laws at weekends. Mum took away my wedding dress, and headdress, for when Peggy was to be married. As Mum said nothing belonged to me in her house, I started to keep everything at the in-laws. I still had to do all the cleaning of the house on Saturday before going to the in-laws.

I left Teignmouth about midday every Saturday, sometimes Friday, if Sid was home for a long weekend. I kept most of my clothes out there now, but I always had to be back at Chapel Street by nine thirty on Sundays. I followed Mum's rules. I still had to do the evening dishes after work. One evening I came home feeling not at all well. I said to Mum, 'I don't want any tea I am going straight to bed, I am not feeling well.' 'Oh no you're not! Do the dishes first.' 'What's wrong with Peggy doing the dishes for a change?' Mum said she was not well. I thought to myself, 'she never is.' Well, so I was getting on with the dishes, when out comes *madam*, and stands by the kitchen door. Peggy was in her fourteenth year now, fifteen at the at the end of the year, and leaving school. Now, Peggy's hands went to her head, she wriggled her fingers saying, 'Na-na-na-na-na!' I couldn't believe it. I thought, 'Why don't you grow up Peggy?' I happened to be wiping a knife, so I just held it above my head, and she was gone in a flash, I had to smile to myself. If that was April, she would have done the dishes for me, that was the difference between the two sisters.

Mother-in-law remarked on how poorly I was looking that weekend. I told her what had happened. Mother-in-law said, 'I suppose you had to clean the house before you left?' 'Yes, of course.' 'Your Mum is working you to death. You are never going to be fit enough to have babies. Why don't you come and live here with us?

When you feel better you can get a job, but do fewer hours, as I know you and Sid want to get a home together.' I said, 'I will think about it. Thank you.' It was July 1954. I didn't know that weekend would change so dramatically for me. Mother-in-law walked to the bus stop that weekend as she always did, but that bus never turned up. We waited for over an hour for the next bus. She was getting anxious, 'Do you want me to come home with you?' she asked. 'No, I am a married woman now, and I must stand on my own two feet. Thank you.' At last the bus turned up. Going home I saw the broken-down bus on Canada Hill, I was going to be an hour late back.

I got home and told Mum what had happened. 'I don't believe you! I know what you have been up to, no good! I don't want any dirty stop-out here!' and she started to thrash me hitting me across the head face and body calling me names. She was like a mad woman, it was awful. I shouted, 'Mum that's enough. Stop! You told me you don't want any dirty stop-outs here, I am not a dirty stop out. Why can't you take my word for a change, instead of calling me a liar, all the time. I am going to bed now. Good night.'

Next day on the way to work I got the Western Morning News, to see if they had any flats in Plymouth. There was one I was interested in so I phoned up at lunch time and asked if I could view it the following day. I then phoned Sid as he had been posted to H.M.S. Defiance, a Plymouth base, for a few months, for training. He met me at North Road Station on the Tuesday, and we went along to look at the flat. It was just right for us. So, we paid the deposit and rent, and were told we could move in on Saturday, which we did. I said to Miss Goff, 'I'm sorry I can't give a week's notice, but living with Mum has become impossible.' 'Yes, I know, but we are sorry to lose you. Good luck to you.' Sid and I moved to Plymouth. I was sad to leave my Teignmouth behind, but what could I do? I had to get as far as I could, away from my Mum. But my Mum's words as I left, 'You will be back!' I thought, 'Don't hold your breath.'

15

Sid didn't stay on H.M.S. Defiance for long. As soon as he finished his course he was back on sea-going ships. In fact, over the first ten years of our marriage I only saw him for about eighteen months. Not much of a marriage. While he was away, he seemed to cut himself off from me, and mostly he only wrote when he was coming home. I got myself a job in a sausage factory. It didn't last long. I felt so sick having to fold this long strip of sausage into eights. I think the factory was called Bowyers or something like that, (during this last year, 2018, I have begun to eat sausages again. I thought I had been turned off sausage for life.) I left there and I got myself a little job three days a week, cleaning a house for very nice people. The money, which was thirty shillings, helped me out, along with the Navy allowance which was four guineas a week. They fed me at my place of work. We had tea or coffee and a biscuit, at eleven o'clock, I also had a cooked lunch at one. This helped me a lot and I managed to save a bit every week.

The sickness was nothing to do with the sausage factory. Before Sid left Plymouth, he had left me pregnant, but I became very ill and couldn't keep any food down. After being ill for about a month, the doctor told me, even after bed rest, I had lost my baby. I went back to my little job. Sid came home on leave, and as I thought he had made me pregnant again I went to see the doctor, as he wanted to keep an eye on me this time. I was sent along to an ante-natal clinic in Beaumont Park. After the doctor there examined me, he asked whether I had been seeing a doctor. 'Yes, he sent me here.' I wondered what was wrong now. The doctor at the anti-natal clinic asked, 'Can you tell me your history over the past six months?' I told him about losing the baby while I was so ill and about my own doctor still insisting that I should stay on my iron medicine for the acute anaemia I still had.

'I can see you are under nourished, and the anaemia is quite serious,' the doctor said. I was still in a size twelve dress, and didn't look pregnant, as I had lost so much weight while I was ill. 'I need you to go up to the hospital right away, to have an X-Ray,' he continued. He gave me an appointment to see him the following week. When the next week arrived, I went along to find the doctor was smiling at me. 'It's good news! I was very worried last week after what you told me. I wondered if your baby was complete. But everything is alright. It looks like you were having twins and lost one. But you have got a lovely healthy baby there, so you've got no worries. You are not three months pregnant, but six months!' he said, still smiling. I couldn't believe what I was hearing. 'Oh, and your baby is due in April 1955. All we have to do is get you built up now.' Before very long the weight went on in leaps and bounds. In April 1955, a week before my baby was due, my brother Colin's marriage took place to Daphne. The wedding was in Shaldon. I was so disappointed I couldn't attend. I was too near my time.

I had let Mum back into my life and told her that I was having a baby in April. It was 1955 now and time was drawing near, and I was taken to a place call Flete Maternity Home, Holbeton in Yealmpton near Modbury. We were taken there a few days before our babies were due because it was so far out from Plymouth. It was a unit that had been opened during the war as Plymouth was badly bombed. I had seen very little of the outside. I think it was a red sandstone place with ramparts. Once a grand old country house, it belonged to Lord Morley, who also owned Saltrum House. At one time Queen Victoria stayed there. I think Flete house was built before dot one, it was so antiquated. We all had a meal. The ladies in waiting told us their stories and while some of them were not too clean, they were funny. They spoke of how they would walk to Modbury with their husbands to have a drink in the pub and what they got up to! Say no more! We laughed so much we were aching. A nurse said, 'It's bedtime,' and they filled up the first ward.

There was only one other lady and me left. We were shown to a great room, it was creepy. There was ivy all around the windows, tap, tap, tapping on the panes. This lady and I looked at each other. 'I am glad we have each other. I wouldn't like to be there on my own.' Then I had a pain in my back. That hurt. Shortly after I had another pain, then another. This lady picked up her watch, 'Tell me when you get another pain,' so she started to time me and told me I was in labour. 'I will ring for the nurse.' She went over to the bell, pulled on it, and ended pulling the whole issue down. 'It looks like I need to find a

51

nurse,' so off she went, leaving me in this creepy room with ivy tapping against the window. She was gone for ages. At last she came back, 'Didn't I have a job to find the nurse!' It was such a creepy place at that time of the night.

The nurse finally came to take me up to the labour ward, to prepare me for the birth. It seemed ages to me waiting on my own in this little room, but it was less than twelve hours from the first pain to the baby being born. Paul arrived at noon on Saturday. He was eight pounds, three ounces. I wept for joy as I held my baby for the first time. This was mine to have and to hold and to love, as I did up until when he died on the sixth of June 2018. He still holds a special place in my heart, he was such a loving child. God bless and keep you safe, my dear, dear Paul.

Some of the ladies came up to see me later on that Saturday. They said it wasn't fair, as some of them had been waiting over two weeks for their babies, but they said that at least I set the ball rolling again, as another lady had just given birth to a boy, and another one was in labour. Soon the wards were full up with mums and babies. On the Sunday, Sid came out with Mum and my stepfather to see me and the baby. Mum was all sweetness, not that mad woman that had beaten me and called me a liar when I got back from Ogwell that awful evening.

16

Mum asked me to come up to Teignmouth for a fortnight when I came out of hospital and before I went home, as Sid was going back to sea. It would be alright if things went wrong as I had my flat to run to. 'Yes, please. One or two weeks will be lovely. I can see my friends and workmates and show off my baby.' I went around to all the departments at the laundry to show off my baby son, leaving the packing room to the last, as that is where I was working at the laundry in the end, as a packer. One of them was counting on her fingers. I said, 'It's alright Bessy, it is one year six days. No, it wasn't a shotgun wedding!' She didn't know where to look, as the other girls were laughing, as she did this to all the young girls. I stopped for a cup of tea so that some of them could have a cuddle with Paul.

Everything turned out fine staying at Mum's. For the first time I felt a part of the family. I would stay at Chapel Street after that, from time to time and Mum would also come and stay with me in Plymouth. They loved Paul, he was such a happy little chap, and he was walking by the time he was twelve months, and he was dry by day, and soon dry by night at just over twelve months. He was a good baby. He loved me to play and read to him, which I did a lot. He also loved the long walks. I would take him up around the Hoe. Paul loved seeing the Sunderland planes taking off from Mountbatten, which we were lucky to see most days. I would walk home through the town and do most of my shopping, where I could buy things that were cheaper, like broken biscuits. I didn't have a lot of money, as you didn't get family allowance for the first child. On our walks I would always finish up at Friary Station before taking Paul home, as that was one of his other loves.

I had paired up with a lady called Jean. She had a little baby called Robert. Jean said, 'I hear your Husband is out in the Suez. What ship is he on?' 'H.M.S. Decoy.' 'My husband is on H.M.S. Ark Royal,' Jean said, 'I hear from him every day. The Ark Royal is picking up all the mail from the ships and taking it ashore.' I said, 'Lovely.' That's all. And quickly changing the subject I said, 'My brother, Colin, is out in Egypt with the army.' As Sid didn't write to me very much, only now and again might I get a letter. When he was on his way home from the Suez he did write just before coming home, telling me that they were not allowed to write home while they were in the Suez. What a lie! In his letter he told me when his ship was coming in, which dockyard to meet him at and the time and which gate. This was the time I started to doubt his honesty.

Some days Paul and I, and Jean with her baby, would have a bit of a change and walk across the Embankment, where we would have the River Plym one side and the trains on the other. Then there was another nice walk into the Saltrum Estate, where we would pass our time. It was a very pretty place with wild fowl on the river and different wildflowers. I thought when the snowdrops were out was the prettiest time of the year. Queen Victoria came up the river Plym and stayed at Saltrum House. Sometimes Jean would come with us, but Robert was a fussy baby and she found him hard work. 'I wish Robert was more like your Paul! He is such a happy baby,' said Jean.

We didn't see a lot of Sid. On one occasion, when he came to Plymouth, he spent a few weeks there as he was on The H.M.S. Guardian before it went into mothballs. The crew's wives and children were invited to spend a day on board. We walked up the gangway and our children were taken away from us. Paul was only nine months then. It was to be a day off for the wives. We were pampered and were taken down so far as the Eddystone lighthouse before we had our lunch. It was splicing the main brace, a drink of rum all way round (not me, thanks!) I can't remember what we had for lunch but there was certainly plenty of it and it was good. Then we had afternoon tea. I also met a Teignmouth girl; one of the Tibbs' family. I can't remember her first name after all this time, but we did meet up a few times in Plymouth later on.

I saw Sid now and again. This time he was on H.M.S. St. Kitts, when he docked in Plymouth. But as it was a sea-going ship he was sometimes away for up to eighteen months or even more. So, mostly it was just Paul and me. But we were very happy. Most of all it was a loving environment. I would read to Paul nearly every day. As I read, I pointed at the words. Unknown to me, by pointing at every word as he sat on my lap, I had taught him to read! This evening I was not feeling too good, I was just reciting the story, still pointing at the words,

'Mummy, you left out a word,' 'What word?' I asked. 'Paul can you read?' 'Yes, Mummy!' 'Well, go on and read the rest to me.' He was in his third year, and word perfect. I thought he was just reciting it, so I picked up the newspaper, read a little from it, and Paul started to read. He stumbled over a few of the words he had never seen in his baby books, but other than that, he could read!

17

It was now coming up to the Christmas of 1957. Sid's leave was not until the New Year this time; our first New Year together in our little home. Jean and her husband came over to us for New Year's Eve, and we went over to their place on New Year's Day. We had a lovely time together. It was to be the last time I would see Jean and her husband, as his time in the navy was up and they were going up line to where her husband lived. Sid had to re-join his ship. He left me pregnant again. In the February 1958, I went up to stay with Mum for a while. Paul was very ill with measles. It was in his eyes, ears and all over his body and he had to be in a darkened room. The doctor came up twice a day at first. My stepfather taught Paul a rhyme: 'Dr Clayton Payne isn't no good! Chop him up for firewood!' The doctor came into Paul's room, and Paul blurted out the rhyme! The doctor looked at me, shaking my head, and pointing at my stepfather, but the doctor smiled. 'It is nice to see the little chap picking up so well!' laughing. 'I'll see him again tomorrow.'

Sid was coming home on Summer leave. We went to spend a week at Ogwell, went down to see Mum for a day, and spent the day on the beach. It was a lovely day out. Then it was time to go back to Plymouth. On the way home Paul got a little restless so Sid started digging around in his pockets for some paper for Paul to draw on. The next piece of paper Sid pulled out was beige with writing on. He tried to put it back in his pocket quickly, but I was quicker than him and grabbed it because I could see it was a copy of his son's birth certificate. I could see there were addresses on the back of it, and I put it in my handbag, and I picked Paul up and cuddled him in. I didn't know if it was comfort for Paul or for me. I was carrying Sid's child and holding Paul in my arms. My heart was breaking. Was he playing away from home?

I laid Paul in his cot as he was sleeping now and took out the birth certificate. Looking at the back of it there were some girls' names and addresses on it. My eyes filled up with tears. Going back into the other room I confronted him. 'This, on the back of your son's birth certificate! It's sacrilege! On your own son's birth certificate!' He tried

56

to make excuses. 'My mates never had any paper, so I wrote their girls' addresses on it.' 'I might be cabbage looking but pull the other leg it's got bell on!' I said. 'I don't believe you! The addresses are all from different places.' I kept the certificate. And Sid went back to his ship.

As my baby was due soon Peggy was coming down early, so that she could take Paul back when the time came. But the time came sooner than expected. That night, I went into premature labour. I got Peggy and Paul on the train, and I carried on to the Alexander Nursing Home. I thought I was going to have the baby in the taxi. A good job I didn't, as things started to go wrong, I had a difficult birth. I stopped pushing. All I could remember was the nurse sticking a needle into the top of my leg.

I didn't wake up until the next day, to find my mother-in-law with her sister Aunt Eve in the room. The nurse brought a baby to me. 'That's not my baby, it belongs to a foreign lady!' The baby was of yellow colour, with a mass of black hair, and almond shaped eyes. 'That's not mine!' and I started to cry. The nurse came over to me to calm me down. 'This is your baby!' She explained to me that the baby, being premature, had jaundice. 'She will go back to her right colour in a few days, she's such a pretty baby. She was seven pound fourteen ounces at birth. What are you going to call her?' I said to the nurse, as she laid this baby in my arms, 'Lydia Jane,' 'Oh that's a pretty name for a pretty child.' But I still had my doubts. I had a chat for a while with my mother-in-law and Aunt Eve, and they had a cuddle with the baby. Then, as it was time for my afternoon nap, they left.

Mum brought Paul back, but I think at first, he was jealous of his baby sister taking up so much of my time. I thought I ought to be careful. 'Paul, do you think you can help me, because your sister takes up an awful lot of my time. Will you get some clothes for her, please?' Into the bedroom he went, 'What colour outfit today, Mum?' 'Pink. Don't forget her vest and nappy.' I got her bath ready and started bathing her. 'Go and get two of your yellow ducks and show her how to play with them!' Bath time became fun. I took her out of the bath to dry her. 'Don't run away! You've got to put the talc on her, be careful, not too much!' Then I got him to help me dress her and put Lydia in the carrycot. 'That was fun, Mum. Can I help again tomorrow?' 'Oh yes, please. Every day!'

The problem was, when we went out, he wanted to catch hold of her hand, his feet were getting tangled with the wheels, so I took his shoes off and sat him in the pram on the way home. I went to a second-hand shop and got a pram seat for Paul. He loved that; he was happy just to be near his baby sister. No more jealousy. Everything I did, I seemed to do right, as both my children were happy and felt loved.

The next big problem was money. I was still only getting four guineas plus eight shillings as a weekly family allowance, as you only had family allowance for the second child, but I managed. What Mum had taught me as a child came in handy. The marrow bone boiled up then left to set the next day, remove the fat to cook with, and you were left with a lovely rich aspic jelly, a couple of oxos, then turnip, carrots, onion, parsnips, and potatoes and you had a lovely stew full of goodness. Paul's old rompers were cut down and turned into dresses for Lydia. 'Waste not, want not,' was one of my Mum's sayings. She was right. It got me though the lean times. I don't know why I kept all of Paul's things. I had been told by the doctor I wouldn't have any more children as I had been back and forwards to the hospital for over a year after having Paul. Something to do with the womb. Although all my pregnancies were very difficult, I went on to have four children. I do think the doctor may have been wrong!

One day, a social worker came around to see how I was getting on. 'How do you manage in this small flat with two small children? The kitchen is not much more than a cupboard!' 'I take them out a lot to parks. Lydia sleeps in the carrycot and Paul in the cot.' The social worker said, 'I will see what I can do for you.' A couple of weeks later she was back again. 'I have got a house for you, out at Southway, I am arranging a lift for you so you can see the place.' She told me when I would be picked up. I was given a lovely new council house, two bedrooms and a bathroom. No more having to have a bath in a tin bath! It had an indoor toilet, a lovely kitchen, a big living room, and a garden at the front and back. I could have wept for joy as the rent was also cheaper than the flat we were in. We moved in just before

Christmas in 1958, God must have been with me that day when the social worker called. 'Thank you!'

I had lots of things given to me when I moved in: a bed for Paul from mother-in-law, curtains from Aunt Eve, mats for the floor and bedding from my Mum. It all helped to start me off, as I already had some of my own furniture at the flat, having bought a little at a time. Everything started to look nice. I planted things in the garden, grew my own veggies; potatoes, as I was told that breaks the soil up; runner beans, peas, sprouts, and other things. I let Sid back into my life, though he never stopped going out with other women. One day I was washing his work shirt, 'What's this in his pocket?' I asked myself. It was a letter to another women, 'Dear Irene, Thank you for a lovely weekend at Whitby....' I couldn't read any more.

18

It was February 1959. My Paul was not well. I couldn't put my finger on it, so I took him to the doctors. He could find nothing wrong with him. A few days later Paul couldn't walk. I carried him downstairs and put him in the armchair to look out the window to watch the children playing on the green, hoping it would encourage him to want to go out himself. But no, he simply went to sleep. I called the doctor in. He tore me off a strip, saying there was nothing wrong with him. 'Haven't you got any other children?' 'Yes, a six-month-old.' 'Well, don't call me again! I won't come.'

That evening I called Maureen my friend in. She said, 'Paul isn't looking at all well.' I told her what the doctor had said. She said, 'What! I can't believe it!' I asked her if she thought it could be flu? 'It might be. I'll get my husband to go down to the chemist and get him some medicine.' We gave Paul a dose, Maureen said she would be over first thing in the morning to see how thing were. That night I took Paul to bed with me, after putting Lydia down. I didn't sleep. I just held him close to me. He was moaning and groaning. He was in a lot of pain. He opened his eyes, 'Mummy hold me close.' I couldn't have been holding any closer. There was something very wrong, as I held him in my arms, I knew I would have to pluck up enough courage to phone that doctor again.

Maureen came over, then she went back for her husband. He said 'I am going over to the phone box for you, Faith. I will phone that doctor and demand he comes up right away. Maureen took Lydia with her saying she would bath and feed her and keep her. I said thank you, laid Paul on the bed, quickly got dressed and got a few things together. The doctor soon came, and taking one look at Paul said, 'I must go out to phone box and phone for an ambulance, I will be straight back. When the doctor came back, he said he thought it was meningitis. How long had he been arching his back? Most of the night, he had been in awful pain. The ambulance came and I went with them. The ambulance crawled to the hospital. No bells, just steady in silence. We reached the hospital and Paul was taken to a little room. The nurse came to me. 'The doctor is going to give Paul a lumbar puncture, I will take all his details while they are doing that.' I was told it was meningitis. He was taken to a ward, and I was told it would be better if I returned the next day. So, I gave Paul a kiss and went home.

I was not home very long before the doctor called me. He was very apologetic, but that didn't take the fear away as I knew my son was very ill. All I could do was to pray to God. I went over to my friend Maureen to fetch my Lydia and filled her in on what was happening and told her about the doctor apologising. Maureen said she would look after Lydia while Paul was in hospital, since she was such a good baby. I told Maureen what time I would be leaving the following day. I got Lydia ready for her feed and bed and when I finished feeding her, I put her in her cot, as I needed to write some letters about Paul; one to my Mum, another to Sid's mum and finally one to Sid himself. I found writing to Sid was very hard, the tears ran down my face as I poured out was happening to our son, and how ill he was. I never had an answer from Sid. I needed to sleep. I went upstairs and looked in on Lydia. I had to pick her up and hold her close to me. But, instead of putting her back in her cot I took her into bed with me and we both slept until the morning.

I returned to the hospital that afternoon not knowing what was in front of me. I was rushed to an office and was told Paul was not responding to any of the known drugs. I was asked if I would agree to try a new drug, '…otherwise your son will not last the night!' I could hear this voice telling me all this, but I couldn't tell you if it was a man or woman. This voice was telling me I had to sign for this new drug to be used on my son. I was not allowed to see him at this stage. He had to be kept very quiet and still. 'You can just see him from the door!' I blew a kiss to him and walked away and was told to come back the next day.

I don't remember leaving the hospital, or going to the bus stop, but apparently, I did, and our bus conductor saw me there. Hc said it looked like I was in a state of shock, just standing there crying, so the bus conductor put me on the bus, and said to the people on the bus, 'I am looking in her handbag for her return ticket and her keys. Can any of you kind ladies passing number 11 see her home? I know this lady has got a very sick son in hospital. What's happening, I don't know. Will you see her safely into her home, and lock her in, and put the keys through the letter box.' When I was late to pick up Lydia, Maureen got worried, so she slipped over to my place, as she had the backdoor keys. She took back what Lydia would need, bathed and fed her and bought her back and put her in her cot. Her husband came with her. They put me on the bed and covered me over, but Maureen kept popping back to keep an eye on things.

I told Maureen what was happening with Paul, 'I don't remember leaving the hospital, and how I got home. Thank you, Maureen, you have been an angel, I don't know where I would be without you, you have been such a good friend.' Maureen said, 'Let's hope you will have better news when you go in this afternoon.' 'I have got a good feeling I will,' I replied. 'That's the way to think Faith!' she answered.

I often had these feelings, so off I went, light of heart and light of step, to find the matron there with a smile on face. 'Your son is now responding to the drugs, but there is still a long road ahead. He is still a very poorly child, but he is responding.' I bent over his cot lightly and bushed his cheek with my lips. It was as if he was in a kind of coma, or maybe it was the strong drugs he was on. I sat every afternoon, talking quietly to him, for about three weeks. Then one day he was awake. He held out one little hand for me to hold. But when Paul did come around, he couldn't talk, walk or feed himself. Mum and my stepfather came down most weekends. Mother-in-law and Aunt Eve also came to visit.

I was asked if I could come in earlier, to feed and exercise Paul, as they were short staffed. 'I will have to ask my friend, as she is looking after my baby.' Maureen said yes, and for the next three weeks I did just that, walking him around the ward and feeding him. One of the nurses came over to me one day. She said, 'I have never before seen such a bond between mother and child, even when he was so ill in his cot, he would get very fussy for about ten minutes before you came through the door. Once you kissed him and held his hand and started to talk to him, he would settle. We all started to time Paul! We swear that child knew when you were coming even before you entered the ward! He is our miracle child and we wish all children had the closeness that you and Paul have.' It was time for Paul to go home. The doctor said, 'His mother can do more for Paul now, than we can!'

The first thing Paul wanted to do was to hold his Lydia. He had missed his baby sister. It was surprising how Paul was back to his old self in next to no time, talking, running and walking, reading, writing, and helping with Lydia. I also think this was the time I realised how many good people there are around. Maureen and her husband for starters. Without their help, I wouldn't have been there for Paul. Then that lovely bus conductor, who put me on his bus, and made sure I got home. That was above and beyond his duty. And the person that saw me into my house. What care they all took of me! I was a very young mother of 24, in distress at that time. In all that time I never heard anything from Sid, he never sent birthday cards to the children, or wrote.

19

It was early 1959, Paul was still in his fourth year. I went down with a bad bout of flu. I could feel it coming on. I got the children ready for bed, and by this time I was really feeling ill. I could hardly stand up straight. How was I going to get Lydia upstairs and in her cot? I couldn't carry her. I knew I mustn't frighten Paul, so I thought for a moment and then I said to Paul, 'We are going to be a family of lions going to our den! Get down on your knees, as we have got to crawl up the stairs.' I was praying to God I would safely get them to bed. Putting Lydia up a stair at a time we got to the top. We crawled across the bedroom. How was I going to get her in her cot! 'Paul, you let down that side and I will let down this side.' I gave Lydia a kiss. I struggled with Paul to help me put her in the cot. Now it was time to get Paul to bed. 'Let's crawl over to your bed, trying to make a noise like a lion!' Paul got into bed. 'Do I lick or kiss you?' 'Don't be silly Mummy!' 'Lions lick their babies,' I said. I gave him a kiss and told him I loved him, and he was laughing at me. I crawled away to my bedroom trying to sound like a lion. I could still hear Paul giggling to himself as I got in to bed. I was pleased I hadn't frightened him.

Apparently, I must have frightened Paul the next morning as he found me on the bedroom floor. I must have tried to see to Lydia in the night and collapsed on the floor. Now Paul, got his baby sister out of her cot, somehow got her downstairs, took off her wet nappy, I don't know if he washed her, and put a dry nappy on her. You must remember they were terry towelling with a big safety pin in then! Then he fed her a bottle of cold milk. How he got the teat on I don't know as it was hard even for me! Then he put her in her pram. Now, how did he get help? Paul couldn't reach the handles or keys to the front or back doors as they were set about three quarters of the way up. All he could do was to sit on the windowsill and wait.

Maureen, my friend, came out to hang out her washing. Paul banged on the window. She looked over to see no curtains drawn and not a window open, as we had to open the windows because they were metal frames, and dripping with condensation, so she climbed over the fence. Paul opened the window so that Maureen was able to get in. She told me later that Paul hardly gave her any time to stand up before taking her hand and pulling her up the stairs, to find me a heap on the floor. She told Paul to stay with Mummy as she needed help. Maureen went back to get her husband to help to get me back into bed, and phone the doctor. The doctor told Maureen that it was a bad bout of flu, plus the anaemia that had plagued me all those years. He wrote out a prescription and asked if I had enough of the iron medicine. Maureen found a big bottle full and the doctor said I would soon be back on my feet.

Maureen phoned my Mum at her place of work, and she said that Theo would be there later to fetch us and take us back to Teignmouth. When I got back from Teignmouth, Maureen said, 'What a lovely little boy you've got, to do what he did that day.' When I picked Lydia up her nappy fell off! We both laughed, but you must give him points for trying. Maureen went on to say there wasn't a mark on her! I looked. How did he got her out of that cot and down the stairs without hurting her? One of life mysteries! That's is all I can say.

I went on to tell Maureen how Peggy has never believed that I had to bath her a few times when I was five years old. I had washed and dressed her many times in the morning. But, believe me or not, I did! It was the way I was brought up. I could do all the jobs Mum asked of me, because she always showed me how and taught me well. I knew Mum depended on me. I was very willing to help. But, even though a little younger, I had let Paul help me and, just by watching me, he had been able to do what he did. Some of us don't give young children enough credit. They *can* learn things at a very early age instead of sitting in front of the T.V. We had to keep our children amused, no washing machine, no cleaner for the floor, no phones, only the richer people would have these things. Our lives were very different. Only four pounds, four shillings, plus eight shillings family allowance a week for the second child to keep the family on! Don't ask me how I did it! I don't know, but I was never in debt.

20

It was now the summer holidays 1959. I was bathing Lydia, and Paul was in the back garden. He wanted a drink of water. Sid wouldn't get off his backside to help me, so Paul ran into an open window in sheer frustration. I whipped Lydia out of the bath, wrapped her in the towel, put her on the floor under the table and ran out to Paul. There was blood spouting out of his head and a big cut just over his lip. I put my hand over the top of his head, thinking it would keep the blood in. Now, the sight of blood was my biggest phobia. I just stood there and screamed my head off. A policeman who lived two doors away jumped over the garden wall and a nurse came from over the other side. Sid was still sat in his chair. I was hysterical, but I wouldn't let Paul go. So, the police slapped me across the face, and I came to my senses. I picked up Lydia and put her in her pram, still wrapped in the towel. The policeman got me to put a finger on a pulse, or pressure point, as the nurse was holding the other pulse. The policeman went to call for the ambulance, which came very quickly, and I went to hospital with Paul. They stitched Paul up, and sent us home.

The in-laws had arrived by the time I got back. I put the finishing touches to the dinner for all of us, as Sid was still on Easter leave. No help from any one and still feeling shaky, I did it all. I took in four dinners, there was just Lydia's and mine to do. I put Lydia's dinner though the sieve, and brought it in with mine, only to find I hadn't brought in Lydia's spoon, so out I go again to fetch it. There was one almighty scream. I ran back to find Sid holding Lydia's face down in her dinner. By this time, she was turning blue. I knocked Sid out the way, grabbed Lydia out of her highchair and took her to the kitchen to wash the dinner off her face. It was in her eyes, up her nose and in her hair. She was in an awful state. I couldn't calm her down. The little mite was so distressed, so I took her upstairs and cuddled her. Up came Paul, 'Is my Lydia alright Mummy?' 'Yes, my love.' But still very upset, he asked, 'Why did Daddy do it?' 'I don't know why,' I said. I put Lydia in her cot and left Paul up with her, reading to her.

I went down to make her bottle. While it was cooling, I went into Sid. They were laughing at something. I said to him, 'What made you do a foolish thing like that?' I was mad with him. He said lamely, 'She was picking her dinner up with her fingers, so I thought I would teach her lesson!' 'You idiot! You could have killed her with the shock of it, I should report you for threatening a baby like that. All you had to do is to move the dinner out of her reach. You can clear all the dishes and wash them up. I am going to give the baby the bottle. If you want tea, you make it yourself.' 'What about your dinner?' Sid asked. 'It's cold. Bin it!'

I was in no mood for eating, so I went upstairs and was feeding Lydia with her bottle. Sid came up shortly with a cup of tea. Lydia's reaction was instant. She spit the teat out and went stiff. She never liked her father from that day onwards, and she always called him '*that man*' never Dad. It didn't matter how hard I tried.

In 1960 Paul started at school. He loved it so much. Even when he was poorly it was a job to keep him home as he didn't like missing any classes. But for little Lydia, she cried for her *All* and I couldn't get her away from the front door. So, I sat on the bottom stairs with her. 'I want my *All,* Mummy.' 'He will be home soon darling. He has got to go to school. He is five now, a big boy.' Although Lydia could speak well for an eighteen-month-old child, she just couldn't pronounce Paul. After a week of this, and knowing Paul was coming back every day, she was her happy self again.

In about the summer of 1960 I was trying hard to make my marriage work. I never felt the same for Sid after that fatal day on the train, the summer of 1958, when I found out that Sid was unfaithful. I went to my mother-in-law and asked if she could have a word with Sid. 'Oh, not my Sid! He could never be unfaithful!' But he was my husband and my vows to God were *for better or for worse*, so I kept on trying, but he continued to hurt me.

Sid came home. 'I have talked to my Mum,' he said. 'We are going to buy our own house. Mum and Dad are going to look after the children, and you can go back to work to help with expenses.' We had to buy a property big enough for the in-laws to have a couple of rooms. I did what I was told, but Sid did not like the idea of my being unfaithful, (which I never was,) but he thought of the idea of bringing his mum and dad to keep an eye on me. I got a job up the road with Ranco making electrical components. Paul was at school by this time and was on his summer holidays. Lydia was about just over twenty-two months; the in-laws came down that weekend, as Sid's summer leave was about to come to the end.

21

Sid went back to his ship that evening as they were sailing the next day, on sea trials, and I had to go to work. Everything seemed to be going well and we soon got into a routine. Paul was still on school holidays. In the meantime, father-in-law found a lovely place; a three-storey house. The next day I looked at it. It was ideal for us all. The ground floor was a flat, which would do for the in-laws and we would have the next two storeys. All we had to do was wait for Sid to come back from sea trials to sign. The next day I was off to work, Lydia was still asleep in her cot. I kissed my fingers and put them gently on her cheek, then went over and kissed Paul. 'See you later, love.'

That morning a chap at work knocked over some boxes with a sack truck, and one of them hit my leg. I didn't think it was badly hurt, but the firm insisted on me seeing the work's doctor, so off I limped. The doctor thought the same, 'I am going to send orders to have a sitting down job for you, as your leg could be back and blue by tomorrow, and painful. If it gets too bad, come back again. I was just going back to work, but I felt I should go home. Why I don't know. One of my feelings.

I crossed the main road and who was coming down the road towards the bus stop, but the in-laws with Paul. I looked puzzled, where was Lydia? When I was in front of them, I said, 'Where are you going? 'To the museum with Paul!' 'But where is Lydia?' 'We don't know. We have not seen her since eight o'clock this morning.' It was nearly twelve o'clock now. 'What do you mean you haven't seen her since eight o'clock?' Something smelt fishy here. Lydia was out of the house by eight! But I didn't leave until quarter to eight and she had been fast asleep in her cot. She wasn't quite two years old.

They were talking about how she could have gone; 'We know she can walk, but she couldn't have opened the door! When she didn't come back, we thought we would take Paul to the museum.' Over my dead body! I caught hold of Paul's hand. 'He is coming with me. And you two can go pack your bags and clear off. I don't want people like

you looking after my children!' I said to Paul, 'Have you seen Lydia?'
'Not since this morning, Mummy!'

Paul and I searched everywhere in the house and out in the back garden. I was worried. She had been missing now for nearly five hours. I went to Maureen's and told her Lydia was missing. We went up the road to the fields. Maureen said she had been out all morning, as she had to see the doctor. We had a good look around the field, but we couldn't find her. I didn't know where to look. 'I think I will phone the police, Maureen!' Maureen said, 'Leave Paul with me.'

As we got to Maureen's path, Molly shouted over, 'Are you looking for Lydia? 'cos, I got her!' She told me that eight o'clock this morning Lydia was sat on her bottom steps crying. 'I asked her if she was lost, thinking she tried to follow you up the road. I picked her up to console her and she just clung to me. When I told her, I would take her back to her Gran's, she nearly went into convulsions. She didn't want me to take me back to *'that horrible woman'*, so I took her in with me as Maureen was out. I just didn't know what to do.' 'It looks like you done the right thing, I can't thank you enough for keeping my baby safe,' and I gave her a hug as I took Lydia from her arms.

I went back to the house. 'Oh, you found her!' said the in-laws. 'Yes! No thanks to you. Have you packed your things yet? 'No, we are not going to until Sid comes back from sea trials and tells us to leave himself, and we are going to take Paul with us.' You are not!' I said. 'We are not leaving our Paul with a slag like you!' they said. 'How dare you!' I said, 'and what do you mean by that?' 'Your dates did not tally with the time our Sid was home and when you had Lydia.' 'You know all about that! You and Aunt Eve were in the room when I kicked up fuss for the reason about the colour of Lydia. When the nurse bought her in, she told all three of us that Lydia was jaundiced because she was a premature baby.' Father-in-law looked at his wife. 'It was your Sid that was playing around, not me, and you will not have it to be. I got proof of it upstairs if you want to see it. Now pack your things and get out of my house, or I will call the police.'

I would have called the police. I didn't want my children in that kind of atmosphere, because it would have been very bitter. I said to the in-laws, 'You can forget about living with us and buying a house. It would have never been worth putting my children in that kind of danger.' As I am writing this, it makes me think, were the in-laws in their right mind? And what happened in the short time? I had left for work at quarter to eight, and Lydia was dressed and outside of Molly's house at eight o'clock. She had been fast asleep in her cot when I left. To top it all, the in-laws never called the police in. When Lydia had been missing for four hours, they were just going off to the museum with Paul. It didn't make any sense to me.

What I think happened is this: Mother-in-law was bullying or cruel to my Lydia in some way, and Paul, loving his baby sister as he did, took her to safety. He would have known the side door was unlocked, which he could open as Mummy just left for work. I think he would have taken Lydia to my friend Maureen's first, found she was out, then taken her over to Molly leaving her on the bottom step. This shy boy would have not had enough courage to go up to Molly's. When Paul saw what he thought was anger on my face he clammed up. It was not anger. It was fear for my child. This is the only thing that was logical to me, and I often wonder if I had had one of *my feelings* that day, which made me turn for home, instead of going back to work like I should have. After this Lydia became a very clingy child.

Lydia was always tripping herself up. She would turn one foot in, then over she would go. I took her to the doctor, and he sent me to the orthopaedic hospital. The doctor said, 'There is nothing much wrong here. It looks like when she is tired she turns her foot in. She should grow out of it. I recommend you go to Clarks shoe shop. Buy her a pair of steel back shoes, and you should find that will do the trick. If it gets worse, come back again. Lydia still continued to trip herself up. I would pick her up and give her a cuddle and kiss it all better, and rub some cream on, and Lydia would always say, 'Mummy has magic kisses.' I personally think it was more to do with the cream I put on. As she got older, it did improve with the steel back shoes.

22

In September of that year 1960, Peggy married Tim. I was maid-of-honour; Jean, then Johns, was a bridesmaid, and Lydia was a little flower girl. She looked so pretty. As we entered the hotel, my Paul took off his cap and someone remarked what a very polite little boy.

Sid left for trials that day, we had no letters, or birthday cards, or Christmas cards. But the children and I wrote to him often. I always made sure the children sent love and kisses to their father, just to let them know they did have a Dad, even if I thought he didn't care about us. I was good at hiding my feelings, caught up in this loveless marriage. I knew I didn't want him in my bed anymore, and we had grown apart, I thought him dirty going out with other women. I was afraid that he might bring something home as he might be coming home soon.

In early 1961 I picked up enough courage to seek advice from the marriage guidance people. I was very honest about my own feelings, and told them about the marriage, and how Sid didn't write except when he was coming home and what mother-in-law was spreading; that Lydia wasn't Sid's. Not a word of truth in it. I told them they could write to Aunt Eve. I know she would verify it for me, as she was there with mother-in-law at the time. And then mother-in-law must have told Sid the same thing, as he asked me if I had been unfaithful to him. I thought, 'What a cheek, this is your mum again!' I said, 'Write to Aunt Eve. Or better still, when you come home, we will have a blood test between you and Lydia. That will settle it once and for all!' The marriage guidance person said, if I took his conjugal rights away, I would be in the wrong and that the best thing was to try for another child. Like a fool, I was willing to try anything to save my marriage.

I had a letter from Sid. 'Will you and the children come to the dockyard to meet me?' It was the first time I had heard from him since he left. I was there, the dutiful wife and mother. After his leave in 1961, he was drafted down to Cornwall, Culdroses. We talked over our marriage. I told him I was very unhappy in the marriage, with the way he cut us off when he went away and didn't bother to write. He told me they were kept busy all the time. 'What?' I said, 'Twenty-four hours a day?' I told him I still wanted him to have the blood test between him and Lydia. He refused. 'Oh, by the way, I went to the marriage guidance people, while you were away. They told me we should have another child; it might help the marriage.' We both agreed, but I had a miscarriage. It was my fault in a way. Now that Lydia's father was home, she became even more clingy. Lydia repeated, 'I don't like that man.' When I told her, 'It is not *that man*, it's your Daddy,' she would still not call him Daddy.

I think this was to do with what Sid and mother-in-law had done, when she was down, and whatever the in-laws did. I would never know. It was locked up in Lydia's little mind. People don't know what damage they can do to a child, and it can stay with them for ever. I couldn't go to the toilet without Lydia knocking at the door. The next pregnancy I had, had to be handled differently. I told Lydia she was much too heavy for me to pick up, so from then on, I would sit down, and she climbed up on my knee, and had all the cuddles she wanted. Lydia was happy with that, but the next pregnancy was very bad right from the start, and all the way through. Towards the end, I could hardly walk, I was in so much pain but not because I was overweight. The doctor couldn't tell what was wrong and from then on, they did home visits.

Sid came home for a weekend and said, 'Good news! We have got a shore base. I am being drafted to Chatham.' 'How long for?' I asked. 'I don't know,' he said. That's when I started to smell a rat. Because we didn't have a house allotted, we had to find a flat. This did not make any sense to me. The forces would have handled me with kid gloves in my state of health. They would have packed up my home, and everything would have been arranged for me but there was nothing. Sid said, 'Pack up your things!' I said, 'You're joking! I am housebound with this pregnancy, I told you in my letter!' Sid looked at me blankly. 'You will have to wait until the baby is born now, I am in no fit state to go anywhere without help.'

Sid said, 'If that is the case, I am going off with Irene, because you are refusing to go with me.' 'I didn't say that I wouldn't go at all. I said, 'At least not until after the baby is born. If you want to go with

Irene, go, and pack your things right away, and don't bother to come back. Our marriage is over. I have worked long enough to try and save our marriage and I failed. It is not worth any more heartbreak.' Three months after, I had my baby. A lovely daughter, Rosie May, was born May 1962,

The midwife came and prepared me for birth. She said, 'We've got a long wait yet, I will make us a nice cup of tea!' But before she could reach the bottom stair, I was shouting for her to come back. She was amazed to find Rosie laying between my legs. She asked if I had a pain. 'No!' I replied, 'she literally swam out when the water broke!' 'I don't know what happened there,' said the midwife looking very puzzled! 'I have never been that wrong before!' As she was cleaning Rosie and me up, she was asking me a lot of question about the pregnancy. I said, 'It will better if I tell you from the very beginning. I was eight weeks pregnant. I lost the baby. I became pregnant very quickly again. I was very poorly all through the pregnancy, but towards the end I became housebound and I was in a lot of pain. I could hardly walk, so the doctor always made house calls. And that's it in a nutshell! She said, 'Your daughter is seven pounds ten ounces! I will go and make that cup of tea now!'

She brought the tea up and sat on the chair bedside me. She was still perplexed. 'You still say you had no pains?' 'That's right.' 'I have never been so wrong before, and I've been on the job for a long time. Now, you said you had a miscarriage, I wonder if all those pains you were getting before, was your bones slowly unlocking, because you couldn't bear your weight very well.' Every day when the midwife came, she would go over to the cot. She would call Rosie her little rascal. 'You were in one almighty hurry to come into this world!' she said. She did turn out to be a little rascal, as well as being very loveable. A lady called Gwen was looking after me at this time, as Maureen had just had her own baby, and Gwen's husband was in the navy, with Gwen also pregnant. I would look after her when her baby was due. That was the way we did things in those days, we looked after each other.

Rosie was a very sickly child. She always seemed at her worst at nights, looking back on it. I think it could have been lactose intolerance. I could never feed any of my babies. As soon I got out of bed my milk just disappeared. Rosie also suffered from bronchitis a lot so, in the end I took her in my bed with me, as I needed my sleep. I put a rubber sheet on the floor, with a pail, also a small bowl of water on the bedside table, and a flannel and towel. To top it all off, I needed to take Lydia in with me too. I did not want her to get jealous. She was still a very clingy child. Next, I had a word with Paul. I told him what I had to do. Paul said, 'I am alright Mummy. I am a big boy now,' He was just seven! '…and I know you love me as well, Mummy.' I gave him a big hug. He was a lovely boy, so understanding, but I loved all my children equally. They were my life and we were very happy together.

23

Money got a lot better when they brought in family allowance for all children. And we voted Mr MacMillan in as Prime Minister, on the promise he would double all forces' allowances, which he did, with the saying, '*You never had it so good!*' Our standard of living changed overnight. No hand to mouth any more, far better food, even some sweets and chocolate and aids in the home for the next three years or more. I slept with the girls. We were all very happy and contented. We went and stayed with Mum for our holidays, so we could go on to the beach. Mum would come with us, so I had a good swim. It was lovely being in the water again. It made me think of my younger days and friends.

Sometimes I would go back for all the summer holidays and work in the laundry again, in the afternoons only. It was owned by Millbay now. They were pleased to see me back. The older ladies said, 'Are you going to get the singsongs started? We missed you when all you girls left.' 'I will have a try, all join in.' So off I go, and started to sing the old song, and taught the girls how to fold the sheets neater. Rene said I had to set the machine to a little faster setting, to keep up with them all. The big boss came in. 'What's going on here?' He couldn't believe his eyes. How neat everything looked! 'Faith is from the old school,' Rene said. 'A happy ship works better.' 'So I see!' he said. 'Carry on girls.' The next day the boss came over to me. 'Will you teach me that song, it's bitsy titsy, or something?' I turned to him pointing my finger at him, I could hardly say for laughing, 'Watch it, we got ladies here, and it is Itsy Bitsy Teenie Weenie Yellow Polka Dot Bikini.' We started singing it for him. 'You have got the words all wrong,' I said to him as he went away, shaking his head. I expect he was smiling to himself though.

We went on holiday with Peggy and Tim a few times. We would go halves in a hire car. That would have been in 1963. Peggy and Tim would stay in Plymouth with us because Tim loved Cornwall, and he did all the driving at this time, as Peggy and I had not learnt yet. In 1964 Peggy gave birth to Dora. When Dora was about eight months old, about May 1965, though I think it might have been a bit later, as the children were on holiday, and things are just coming back as I am writing this. I remember Lydia was up at Teignmouth with Mum, and Peggy and Tim brought her back with them. Lydia stayed with her Aunt Peggy for one night, because they wanted an early start the next day. It had to be the 31st of August 1965, as Peggy had a birthday cake made for Lydia's seventh birthday, and Tim's birthday was the next day, so one half was pink the other half was blue.

The next morning, on Tim's birthday, they came down to pick us up; Rosie, Paul, and me, plus the picnic hamper I had packed with all the goodies. We went to Looe for the day. We got down to a little cove, a beautiful sun trap. I made sure my children and I kept plenty of sun cream on because we were in and out of the water. I gave the sun cream to Peggy and told her to do the same. Tim and I were playing with my three children, in and out of the water and rockpools, only going up the beach for food and drink. We were having the time of our lives splashing each other, but we couldn't get Peggy anywhere near the water. All the family call Peggy *killjoy* as she would never join in any of the fun, shame. Tim was mad with Peggy, as Dora was sun burnt. I had left the sun cream with Peggy; she didn't seem to have put any on. Dora cried all that night. The next day they went home. The holiday had been spoilt and we never ever had any more holidays together with the children.

I had a letter from the council saying I was being allotted a three-bedroom house, that an inspector would be calling around, and the date to expect him. He went up into the loft and bought down a kitbag. 'This must belong to you?' I said thank you. It had to be Sid's, as this was a new house when we moved in. When I opened it was filled with old clothes and unopened letters. I put the unopened mail in a box and binned the old clothes. The inspector said to me, 'You have kept your home in good condition, in fact it is so good, we can move the new people in right away without doing anything. We don't do this very often. You should hear from us in about a week's time and get the new keys.'

I had the new house in late 1965. Next door was another naval wife. We hit it off right away. But the next door up was another kettle of fish. She took an instant dislike to me, only because I was a woman on my own and so she thought I would be after her husband. No way. Her husband and I would often talk over the garden fence, because we were both keen gardeners. Sadly, the soil was not very good for growing, it really needed topsoil and we all ended up just grassing it.

Now Vi, living next door, had three girls. Two of them were older than my children, but Vi and I got on well, always in and out each other's houses. I was careful to keep my distance when her husband was home on leave, out of respect, but most evenings Vi spent her evening with me. As my Rosie was a live wire you just couldn't put her to bed. She just ran until she dropped. You didn't know where you were going to find her; in the bath, in a drawer, in a cupboard, or under one of the beds. I would just pick her up and put her to bed.

I went to the doctor and asked his advice. He said I could put her on drugs for hyperactivity. I said I didn't want her on drugs and the doctor said I was doing the right thing. 'Just keep doing what you're doing. She will grow out of it one day!' the doctor said, smiling. I said, 'Yes, when I am old and grey!' and we both laughed. I had changed doctors. With the estate growing we now had two doctors, and as it happened, this one came from Teignmouth. He worked under my old doctor from Teignmouth, and he always wanted to talk about my hometown. While I could hear Rosie running, it was ok, it was when she stopped, and you went looking for her to see what she was up to, my peace was shattered.

After having two such placid children, Rosie was a whizz bomb. But she was such a loving child. She would run into the room; I don't think she knew how to walk, she would jump up on my lap, put her arms around my neck, give me a big kiss, and as she was getting down she would say, 'I love you Mummy' and she would be gone. I had to smile. One day she was too quiet. I went to see what she was up to. She was on the bottom stair, pulling legs off a spider. I asked her what she was doing that for? 'To see how many legs it can walk with!' was her reply. When she had pulled all its legs off, she swatted it.

Another time she dropped a little china ornament from the bedroom window. It belonged to Lydia. Lydia was in tears. I was very cross with Rosie, 'Why did you do that?' 'Mummy, to see if it would bounce like my ball.' You had to believe her. From the look on her little face, it was clear she was so near to tears herself. 'You'd better say sorry to Lydia.' So, she put her arms around Lydia and gave her a kiss. When I told Rosie about this later in life, she said, 'Well, I was a budding scientist, Mum!' She did turn out to be a scientist. I think it was just an inquisitive mind, not malice. It is very hard being a mother to know when to chastise, but I didn't think she meant to break it, Rosie was not like that.

24

The next thing that I can remember was when she was a little older, just gone three. It was a lovely sunny day and most of us mums were outside watching our children and talking to each other. Now you must remember Rosie was only about three years old. I looked up the street. She was with Paul. That's alright or so I thought. I turned to talk to Vi and the next minute I could hear my Rosie coming down the street, '...*whee*...' She was on Paul's full-size bike. She was sat on the saddle, just about able to put her fingers tips on the handlebars, and her legs spread-eagled. You've never seen me move so quickly. I tried to grab the saddle, but I missed it as she sailed on down the hill, with me running after her. Luckily, she hit a grass turf and came off. Thank God! If she carried on down the grass bank, she would have had a six-foot drop onto the main road! As you can see, I needed eyes in the back of my head. She was not hurt. At that age they don't see fear, and they are more relaxed.

I asked her, 'How did you manage to get on Paul's bike?' 'I got a boy to help me. I climbed on the wall, and the boy held the bike. I got on the saddle and put my fingers on the handlebars and off I went!' 'Well, don't ever do it again. You could have killed yourself.' 'Sorry Mummy.' That child was going to be the death of me. But thinking back she reminded me of myself, when I use to come down over Dawlish Hill holding my saddle instead of the handlebars, when I was about ten, and other silly things. I will not write about laughing to myself. Vi came in that evening and asked where Rosie was. 'Gone to bed for the first time!' She knew she had over-stepped the mark that day.

One day I was tidying one of the cupboards when I came across a box. I opened it up and it was all these unopened letters I had found in the kitbag. I had forgotten about them. I thought I would have a look at it that evening when the children were in bed. Vi came in as I was carrying in the box. 'What's this?' Vi asked. 'It's what Sid left behind. Some dirty clothes in a kitbag up in the loft of the other house. I found them this afternoon while tidying the cupboard, so I brought them in to peruse,' 'That's a posh word for you, Faith!' said Vi. I had learnt it that morning from a clue in a crossword. After reading a few letters, which were mostly from me, 'Oh Vi, read this one,' I said. There were tears in my eyes. 'It's another one from you, Faith!' 'I know, it's telling him about Paul, when he was so ill with meningitis, I can't read any more, it's too painful.' 'Faith, I can still see your tear stains on the paper!' 'Yes, it was the hardest letter I ever had to write, as it was about our son, and how he might not make it through the night. I needed Sid so much that day, and he didn't even bother to read it, no wonder he looked blank at me sometimes.' Vi said, 'How hurtful, what a cruel man. To think, other men would have loved to receive letters like these, so loving, and the little notes on the bottom from the children.' 'Yes Vi, it was my way of letting them know they did have a father, as we didn't see Sid very often. After this I put in for a divorce for desertion. I saw a solicitor. He took all the details and said it would be filed right away. A little while after I had a letter from mother-in-law saying Sid wanted to see the children. So, I wrote back what time and place and she wrote back. Breton Side bus station, eleven o'clock. I can't remember the date after all this time. She said they would bring the children back at five o'clock to Southway, but I was a bit apprehensive, not knowing if they would bring Paul back, as mother-in-law had said she wanted him.'

I showed Vi the letter mother-in-law had written. 'What a cheek,' she said. 'After all this time, he didn't care two hoots about you all. All those unopened letters prove it. I hope you have kept all those letters?' I told her I had. I arranged to see my friend, Beryl, that day, as we had not met up for a while. She lived down the end of Union Street. So, after dropping the children off to mother-in-laws, off I go to my friend Beryl's. When I got there Roger, her brother, was there. A few months before I had put Roger and his mate up for a few weeks for Beryl. She knew I was not using the girls' bedroom, and she didn't have room for two of them. But they soon went back to Bristol, as they couldn't find work down here. Beryl gave me lunch; we had a long talk about what the children had been up to. I told them about Rosie. They laughed, with Roger joining in now and again. It was no laughing matter. She will be the death of me. About two o'clock I was getting a feeling I should be home.

'Sorry Beryl, I got this feeling I must go home!' I said my goodbyes, and off I went. I got home just before three. The three children were running around like little mad things, screaming their heads off. I had never seen such bad behaviour from them, or shall we say the two older children. They were normally so placid, more than I could say for Rosie. Most probably they fed them on rubbish fast food, that might have explained their behaviour then. I calmed them down and I asked how they got into the house? All I could get out of them was that Daddy had lifted one of them up. What I think could have happened was that Sid lifted Lydia, to put her arm though the little kitchen window, to open the latch on the big window, and then put Rosie through the big window, as she was more agile, to open the front door. 'Did your Dad and Gran come in?' 'No, they just left us.'

There was a knock on the door. I opened it. There was a lady standing there. She said, 'I am from Child Welfare, we have had a complaint about you leaving your children.' 'Please, come in,' I said. 'Would you like a cup of tea?' 'Yes, please.' she said. I showed her into the kitchen, so we could carry on talking while I made the tea, then I took her into the lounge because it was more comfortable. I told the children to go up into the bedroom and play with their toys, so that I could talk to the lady. I told her I was getting a divorce, and Sid and his mother had wanted to see the children. I added that we had arranged for me to take them into Breton Side that morning, and that they had said they would bring the children back by five o'clock. 'I popped in to see a friend for a while. As you can see, I was back here by three, as it only just gone three now.' She looked at the clock and nodded. 'Can I see the letter?' 'Yes!' I said. 'I will go and get it. Would you like to see the children on your own?' Yes, please,' she said. So, I called the children down and I left her there talking to the them, while I looked for the letter. Then I remembered I must have left it at Beryl's my friend.

She finished talking to the children. 'Sorry,' I said, 'I must have left the letter at my friend's, but if you need to confirm it, I am sure Vi will be willing to confirm it for me, as she knows my inner most feelings. She lives the next door down. I know she is home. I saw her coming home while I was making our tea.' The lady said, 'If you don't mind, I will.' And off she went. She was gone for a while. When she came back, she said, 'Everything is alright. You've got no worries at all.' But she said she couldn't tell me who had complained. I said 'I know who it is. The women the other side of me thinks I am after her husband. The last thing I want at the moment, is another man. But Sid and his mum won't have the children again in a hurry!' She smiled and said goodbye.

25

Next thing, I got cold feet about the divorce. I kept on thinking *for better or worse*, that was my vows, and the children needed a father. So, I wrote to Sid and sent it to his last known ship. It would find him. Vi said, 'You're being stupid, Faith. A leopard doesn't, change his spots.' 'Vi, I have got to try for my children's sake.' Vi said, 'It will all end up in tears.'

I soon had a reply to my letter, and one Saturday Sid came to see me. We talked things over. I said, 'You must read all my letters.' He looked at me. 'Yes, the inspector found your kit bag, with all the unopened letters I wrote to you, when we were moving house. No wonder you looked at me blank sometimes. We both agreed to try again, for the children's sake. While we were sorting out how to make the marriage work, Sid announced he was off to Singapore. He would be gone for the next eighteen months. Again, I cannot remember times and dates, I would think about 1965 then. So, I stopped the divorce proceedings. Then I waited and waited, for mail that never came.

It was arranged before Sid left for him to see my younger brother Theo and wife Amelia. They were in Singapore. Time went on. There were two airmail letters on the mat. I opened Sid's letter, which said he was sorry he was unable to write, as all the way out they were on exercises. Gwen, the lady who had looked after me when I had Rosie, said this was not true. Her husband, Jim, was in the navy so she knew they didn't exercise like that. 'He is telling you a load of poppycock,' she had told me. 'He should have plenty time to write. Other husbands wrote to their wives, even in the war. Also, what you said, about when your Paul was so ill and you were all on you own, The Forces would have moved heaven and earth to get him home. There is no way they would let you stand on your own like you did. But we know the reason for that was the unopened letters in his kit bag. While Sid was at Singapore, I went to see Theo and Amelia every day.'

I started to read Theo's letter, as all of our family wrote to each other, and we saw as much as we could of each other. Reading Theo's letter, he said 'I just found out Sid's ship just left Singapore, and we haven't seen hide or hair of him. We are a bit disappointed as we had bought your children some presents and we were hoping he would take them, as he should be home before us. It was a good job they didn't give him the presents as I never saw him again. I wrote to Sid saying, 'You fooled me again. So, you will not hear from me again, only from my solicitor. It is over.'

Vi had said she thought it would end up in tears and I had told her I had to try again for my children's sake to save my marriage. In fact, I think in my heart it was for my own beliefs, *for better or for worse*. A few months after, my naval allowance stopped coming from Sid, so all I was left with was the family allowance, and some savings, to feed us, and keep a roof over our heads. 1966 was the worst year of my life. I didn't know which way to turn. I followed what Mum had done. I went to work. It was the wrong move as it happened as I found out later about the D.H.S.S. But I didn't know any better at that time. It was the way I was brought up.

I needed a baby minder for Rosie. Paul and Lydia were at school. I got a job back at Ranco, so all was set. Rosie was a lot better at nights, and I was getting a bit more sleep, but I still slept with the girls, just in case Rosie had a bad night. I was struggling with my bills. I could still just about pay my rent, gas and electric, plus baby minder. But I needed to cut back on my food, sometimes only having the scraps off the children plates. I think I had everything covered, and everything was working out fine. This went on for a few months.

I picked Rosie up on my way home from work. We had a meal, I bathed the children, I did my washing by hand, as I had no washing machine, got the clothes out ready for the next day, and prepared the meals for the next day as well. I did as much cleaning of the house as I could, then I had a bath before going to bed just in case I got up late, which I never did, lucky for me. I just fell into bed, always gone midnight. It was July coming up to the school holidays. The baby minder said she couldn't have Rosie for the school holidays because she had six of her own children to look after

I wondered what I could do! I did not want my Mum to know. Both brothers were away in the army, so that left only my sister April to ask. I wrote to April, and she said 'Yes. When the time comes, I will

85

fetch them, because I want to find out what's wrong! I have a feeling you're not telling me everything.' She was a dear, always there for me. I told her my plight, between Sid and me, and I told her I did not want Mum to know. That meant Peggy as well, as you know what she's like towards me. She would be the first to run to Mum with glee to tell her. She gave me a big hug and kiss and promised to keep the news between herself and Bert. I knew that with April and Bert my children would be alright. I arranged to send them money every week for their keep, as they had six children of their own. There was not much to spare on a farm labourer's money. They were very poorly paid.

For the first few weeks everything went alright. But there was very little money left over to feed me, but I had to send money to April. Then I started to feel ill. But I still went to work. One day, I collapsed. They called an ambulance and took me to hospital. The doctor said I was suffering from nervous exhaustion and was very under nourished. I needed to go to Moorfield Hospital Clinic, so that they could sort my problems out. I said, 'Doctor, I can't. My young daughter is being brought back. She is very poorly. She has got bronchitis.' 'That is alright,' he said. 'A hospital car will take you home, as you will need clothes, for you and your little girl. They will wait until your little girl is with you and you will both be brought to Moorfield.

I went to Moorfield Clinic with my little Rosie. She was very poorly this time, with bronchitis. I hardly left her side, only when I had to see the doctor myself. I was allowed to give her all her medicine, but I had to take the bottle back to the nurse every time, hospital rules. When I did see the doctor, he was asking me all sorts of questions, including why I didn't go to the D.H.S.S.? I looked at the doctor blankly. I didn't have a clue what he was talking about. All I knew was that, even if I was feeling poorly, Mum would send me to work. I think she would have sent me to work even if I was dying on my feet. The other questions he asked, was mostly about my childhood, or marriage. The doctor said, 'I am sending for the Naval Welfare.' I had never heard about them. 'They should be able to sort you out,' he reassured me.

26

Rosie was on the mend now. She was really spoilt there with everybody making a fuss of her. The Naval Welfare came and with them more questions about my marriage. They were so nice. I was able to open up. I explained how, when he went away, he had just cut himself off from us. When he was in the Suez, he said he was not allowed to write home, but that had been a big lie. I told them how my friend's husband was on the Arc Royal, and Jean had told me they were picking up mail from the ships there. So, I had told Jean a lie, that I had received some letters, but I never had. I also told them about the kit bag, and all the unopened letters, and in it was the one about Paul being so ill. They were horrified at what I was telling them. I went on to tell them about the so-called married quarters at Chatham. They said they were glad I never went; they were not married quarters. 'I don't know what he was up to, but you are right, you would have been issued with a house. And you say you were pregnant at the time?' I told them I had been six months pregnant and ill, and that that was when he went off with another woman, and that I didn't see him then for nearly three years.

I told them how I tried to make a go of my marriage again, and that the same thing happened. The Naval Welfare officer asked, 'Do you think you could try again if we got you married quarters, and when he is on sea-going ships, we will arrange for him to take a letter to the Captain once a week, and the Captain will drop it in the post bag. Would you go back with him then?' 'No! Firstly, I wouldn't put him through that shame. If a man doesn't want to write, that's up to him. And you can't make him read my letters, can you!' They had no answer for that. 'No, I will not go back to him now; too much heartbreak, and I can't trust him anymore.'

'We have got some good news for you,' they said. 'You are getting your Naval allowance back right away, plus back pay. We have been working hard for this day, when service men can no longer take their support away from their families leaving them destitute, as your husband has left you.' 'Thank you very much, that is good news.' Within days it came to me, and I was able to go down the village and get some money. I sent some right away to April. The next day the doctor sent for me, 'That was some good news from the Naval Welfare! Did you enjoy it down the village? 'Yes, it was lovely. Rosie and I enjoyed it.' 'You do know you can go out any time you like? There are buses down to the village. You can even go to Plymouth for the day. It is up to you, but I would like you to stay a little longer as we have a little problem with your mother. When she came down last weekend with your two older children, she wanted me to sign a letter to say you are an unfit mother. I know that is not true as I saw the way you nursed Rosie when she was ill, and when your two older children came to see you. I watched you hug and kiss your children and saw how happy they were to see you. Such a happy little family. You could almost feel the love coming from you all, and how sad you all looked when it was time to part. You could see that you didn't want to be parted. I promise you, your mother will not win. We will leave no stone unturned to stop her, so don't you worry.'

I had a letter from April, saying I had sent her far too much money, as Mum took Paul and Lydia away from her, and she hadn't been able to stop her. She had also had the welfare around there. But as the doctor promised, I was soon home with all my children. Vi was pleased to see me back. Shortly after, I told Vi how Mum had tried to take the children away from me, funny really, since I never told Mum about Sid and me breaking up.

It was coming up to the end of the summer. Paul had passed for high school. He was going to Sutton High for boys, one of the best schools in Plymouth. I had a list of clothes to buy for him. We went into town and got everything on the list for Paul. 'Next time we will get you new clothes, Lydia.' 'What about me, Mummy?' asked Rosie. 'You're too young yet. I will buy you some new clothes and shoes when they go back to school. Alright?' In the meantime, I had a letter from Mum. 'They are going to pull down Chapel Street. I am going to be rehoused! I have been thinking! Now you are on your own, would you like to share a house with us? We could go in for a four bedroomed house. You can have three bedrooms. Your stepfather and I could have the other room. We could turn the dining room into a lounge so that we can have a lounge each and share the kitchen. You would pay three quarters of the rent and three quarters of the utility bills.' I thought that was fair. And I always wanted to go back to Teignmouth. I still had great faith in Mum, that she wanted to help the children and me.

There was one snag though. Paul was going to Sutton High. It was a very good school and it put me in a bit of a dilemma as to what to do. I talked to Paul. I told him I was getting a chance to go back to Teignmouth but that I also wanted him to go to Sutton High. 'I have been thinking how to get around it,' I said. 'Paul, you can't miss this chance, it such a good school. What about if Mary, my friend, could take you in. You would stay there on weekdays and come home at weekends and holidays. What do you think?' 'It could work Mum. We could go down to Mary's and ask.'

We arranged to see Mary and her husband. They always wanted children but were never blessed. They jumped at the chance of having Paul. They took him to see his room. They couldn't thank me enough. I think it should had been the other way around. I took Paul down to Mary and Bill's to get settled in. A few days before going to Teignmouth I went to say goodbye to Beryl who was there with Roger. I told them I was going back to Teignmouth to live and said my goodbyes. As I was about to leave, Roger said 'Can I come up to see you now and again?' I couldn't say no, as Beryl had been such a good friend. I was not a bit interested in him, or any other man. How could I ever put my trust in men again?

This was my biggest mistake of my life. I should have kept my house going in Plymouth until I was sure I was doing the right thing. But without thinking straight, I gave up my home and put my furniture in store and left for Teignmouth, and put my trust in Mum, as she had been so different over the last eleven years.

27

It was now September 1966 and I had just arrived back in Teignmouth. I had not been here for even a day before Mum was on me like a ton of bricks. She laid down the law and all my dreams were shattered. 'First, you must do everything I say, with no back answers. Then I will have your Naval Allowance and your family allowance.' I had kept my home running on this for the four us and could save a little every week. She said, 'I haven't finished yet. You can also go out to work full time. And I will have most of that. I will leave you enough to buy new clothes and personal things for you and the children when I think it is necessary for them. I will control all your money.'

I thought how extortionate. 'Plus, you will have to clean the house from top to bottom.' I was thirty-one. I would be thirty-two in two months' time, and here she was treating me as if I was a child or shall we say a servant. I went to speak. Mum said, 'I haven't finished yet.' I wondered what more she wanted of me! 'Paul will leave school in four years' time. He can go to an army apprentice school and give me an allowance.' She meant to *her* not me, like Colin and Theo did. 'But Mum, he will not be accepted in the army. He is stone deaf in one ear, because of an illness.' 'Oh, they won't find that out,' Mum said, 'Only if you tell them.' 'Of course, they will. When they get his medical records, which will go with him. Anyway, he is my child, not yours, and he is staying at school until he has done his O and A levels. Then I hope he will be going on to university.'

'Who do you think you are, going above your station?' my Mum said. I replied, 'Paul has got brains, and they are to be used.' 'No, they are not. Under my roof you do what I say! And Lydia will go in the laundry and work and I can have the bigger part of her wages too, and Rosie is too young to talk about yet.' This was like waving a red rag at a bull. I thought what I have done? 'Please God, help me.'

I said, 'Have you finished? They are my children not yours Mum. I came up here to share a house with you, and pay my share, which I thought was fair, on what we agreed on. I have no intention of doing what you are saying, and the children are going to stay at school until they are eighteen.' Mum said, 'We will see about that! You're living above your station.' 'I don't know what you mean by that. You just won't move with the times. You are too Victorian.' Mum just said, 'I've got you over a barrel, with nowhere to run.' Why didn't I listen to Vi, when she warned me my Mum was up to no good? When she tried to take away my children, when she was in hospital, all she wanted was for the children to keep her in her old age, and most likely work them to death as she did me.

Every day I was out looking for accommodation, but as soon as I revealed I had three children, they turned me down. I left no stone unturned, to find a place. I had a letter from Roger, Beryl's brother. Would I phone him, as he would like to come up and see me? He gave me a telephone number and a time. So down I went, to the phone box and arranged to see him the next day. I would meet him at the station. I took Rosie and Lydia with me. As soon as he saw me, he asked what was up. I told him I would tell him when we were on the beach. It was a lovely September day and I had packed us up a lunch. While the two girls were playing, I told him everything. I asked if he could look for a flat in Plymouth for me. He said he would.

After sitting there talking for a while, he asked, 'What about you and me getting together? I've got a job. We could get a flat. It should be easier if you got a man. You said your divorce should be through soon. We could get married, and you could sleep with the girls until then. I would sleep in another room.' I said, 'There is one snag about that. I don't love you!' 'Well, I got enough love for the two of us!' he said. 'And I promise to see your children are educated as you want them. If it doesn't work, I will just move out. I can't be no fairer than that. If it works, I only ask you to have my child.' What Roger said sounded very fair.

I only thought of the children. If I stayed with Mum, she would ruin their lives. 'Let me sit quiet for a while, Roger please. Just watch the children play for now. It is a big step for me.' I realized that Beryl, his sister, had been trying to match-make all this time. I suggested we could have our lunch and he said he would get a pot of tea. My thoughts were working overtime. I just wanted to say no. The thought of another marriage! Please someone, help me. This was the last thing I wanted. We ate our sandwiches and chocolate bars. Roger bought lemonade for the children and tea for us, then we played with the children, paddled, and made sandcastles together. There was a lot of laughter as Roger swung the children around. I thought I had never seen their own father ever play with them like that. It was lovely. I felt so very relaxed. It was time for Roger to catch the train back to Plymouth. As we were walking down to the station Roger said, 'What's the answer?' 'Find us a flat, please. I will come back to Plymouth.' Roger said, 'That's good.' 'Will you phone me tomorrow about twelve?' I asked. 'Yes!' 'I will wait by the phone box for your call. Alright, bye!' When I got to the house it all started up again. 'Where have you been?' 'Out with the children!' 'You should be looking for work, and by the way, Paul is not coming up every weekend, only holiday times. It is a waste of my money.' 'It is not your money, Mum. It is mine.' Mum said, 'I told you before, everything in this house is mine! Now give it all to me,' she demanded. 'No! I will give you a fair keep, and that's all,' I said. Mum was getting very greedy. 'I have only been here a few days. I have bought our own food, and some of yours, as I have done all the main meals.' 'You didn't today,' she said. 'Yes, I did. You had cold meat and bubble and squeak,' I said, 'and who sent you money every week when Roy was in hospital?' 'Not you!' Mum said. 'You know I did. Two pounds, every week.' 'You're a liar,' Mum said. I retorted, 'I know that my other siblings didn't, because they told me I was a mug to give it to you, because you weren't going to see Roy like you promised.'

Mum said, 'Don't forget you've got a pile of dishes in the sink to wash.' 'No, I haven't. I left the place clean and tidy when I left this morning with the children. We have just come in the door. I am not your servant Mum. It looks like I will have to seek help from the Naval Welfare and get out of here as soon as I can.' For the next few days I was looking hard for a place of my own, but they were either too dear, or didn't want children. I would have loved to settle back in Teignmouth, but to be sensible, it would be better to go back to Plymouth, and to be with my Paul. I was missing him already.

Every day I went to the phone box to speak to Roger. We took it in turns to pay. That day he phoned. 'I have managed to get a large caravan on a farm at Yelverton. It's a start, Faith. There is a double bed for you and the girls one end, which folds back in the day and the same down the other end for me. What do you think?' 'Yes, take it! I will be down tomorrow. I can't take any more here with Mum's nonsense. She just doesn't give up nagging me for more money and to get a job. It is a good job she doesn't know I've got savings. We will need that for a deposit for the flat and to get the furniture out of store. We need to hang on to what I have.' 'Don't forget, I got money too,' said Roger. 'I'll be helping. See you tomorrow afternoon at North Road Station.' 'I will be on the train about one o'clock. I should be there by two,' I replied. It was as if a great weight had been lifted from me.

I was only in Teignmouth for about three weeks. It was now the end of September 1966. As soon as I got back to Mum's house, she demanded, 'Have you got a job yet?' 'No Mum, and I am not likely to for a very long time. I've got a full-time job bringing up my children, and I am going back to Plymouth. I am leaving tomorrow.' 'You can't!' Mum said. 'I can and you can't stop me. You are the one that went back on her word. I didn't like you treating me like I was a child, or shall we say a servant. I am in my thirties now, Mum.'

To top it all I added, 'You are trying to take away my rights as a mother, and you're not going to do it. My children are going to be educated. I want them educated, so they can get better employment, and hopefully, a better life. (Paul became an engineer, Lydia became an office girl in 1972, and is still at the same office in 2019, shortly to be retired, and Rosie was a scientist for twenty-two years, then went on to Welfare work. All three children to be proud of!)

28

Let's get back to 1966; I'm running away with it again. So, I was back again in Plymouth, not knowing what fate awaited me there. The caravan was on the outskirts of Plymouth, a bit small after living in the house. Roger slept at one end and I slept the other, with the two girls. Paul still had to stay with Mary and Bill. This was to be our home for the next month. We were happy in the caravan. The two girls loved it there, but not when the big pig got under the caravan, scratching his back! We thought the pig was going to tip the caravan over with us in it! Then there was the time the two girls put the hens in with the ducks. The cockerel didn't like that, so he pecked Rosie's bottom, and she didn't like that and came in crying. I give her a cuddle and suggested she didn't mess with hens again. Rosie gave the cockerel a wide berth after that. When Roger came back from work, and I told him, we had a good laugh. 'That will teach her!' 'Do you think so?'

One day the farmer's wife knocked at the door, 'There is a phone call for you.' It was Mary. 'There is a flat going in Old Laira Road, Come quickly!' I left a note for Roger, just in case he got back from work before I could get back. We put our coats on, and off we went up the lane for the bus. We got to Mary's and she took us across the road to the flat. I looked at the flat. It was small, but we could manage, and the price was alright. 'Yes, I will have it.' I turned to the landlord, 'I can give you what I have on me, but I need to go to the bank to get the rest.' The Landlord said, 'When you come in tomorrow to sign the agreement, pay me the lot then.' I arranged to get my furniture out of storage and moved in at the weekend. It was the end of October 1966, after settling Lydia, at Laira Green School.

I made arrangements to see my solicitor that week, to see how my divorce was going. 'Sorry, but your husband won't sign the papers. He sent them back unsigned. He sent a note that when you agreed to take him back, you slept together that day.' What a lie! No way, and if he had to pay for the children until they were sixteen, we might as well have stayed married. 'So, I had to change your divorce from desertion, to a divorce for irretrievable break down, because you agreed to give him another chance.' 'I did, and within a few months it had fallen apart with his lies again. Does this mean I am tied to him for the rest of my life?' 'I am afraid so,' the solicitor said. I said thank you and went back to the flat.

That evening, after the girls went to bed, I told Roger what the solicitor had said. Roger said, 'What ever kind of man did you marry? He seems to have no feelings except for himself.' 'Oh, I worked that one out. You're right, to the point of saying he didn't have any feelings. I was to become his home base, just somewhere to come home between ships. I had the feeling that he didn't always come home to me, I think he stayed with other women sometimes.' I was pouring my heart out to Roger, 'Sid would say I was dogged but faithful, I don't really know what he meant by it.' Roger said it could mean like a dog being faithful to his master.

The other thing Sid told me while I was seeing to the baby's needs was, 'Why can't you put that confounded baby down, and spend a bit of time with me?' I said, 'Babies come first. They need feeding washing and changing. You could help me a bit, but no, you just sit there reading. I have to see to the children, do the cooking, cleaning and your dirty washing. I am not your servant; I've only got these two hands. Why did you give me children if you didn't want them?' 'To keep you faithful, and you couldn't even do that.' 'Oh, not that again. Lydia is yours! Get a blood test! It will stop this nonsense. That was your mum turning nasty. When I asked her for help, when I found you were being unfaithful to me, your mother said you could never be unfaithful.' I looked at Sid, and he just grinned at me. My blood boiled. I had never felt so angry in my life, I felt I could wipe that grin right off his face. But the baby started to cry. I turned around and picked her up and cuddled her, holding her close.' I carried on telling Roger my story, how I kept taking Sid back, and how I came to have Rosie. You know the rest.

Roger said, 'Do you want me to leave?' I said, 'Please, give me some space. We don't want to be too hasty. I must think it through first.' I just didn't want to hurt him. Roger went to his bed and I slept with the girls. Roger went to work the next day. I took Lydia to school, and Rosie and I went for a walk. All the time I was tossing around in my head what I should do. We were so happy in the caravan, and Roger was so good with the girls, we seemed like a family. It was a lovely feeling. A feeling I never had with Sid. Roger had helped me so much to get out the of Mum's grip. He helped me get this flat. Would I be able to keep it if Roger went? I couldn't go back to Mum. I prayed and prayed. What was I going to do?

If I stayed with Roger, he would want his own child, and this child would be born out of wedlock. But he promised my children would be educated. Again. I prayed for guidance for the answers. But I was on my own. That evening, right or wrong, I said yes to Roger. I didn't have the heart to keep him on a piece of string any longer, but I found it hard to live with my conscience. It didn't come easy because of my faith, and I was breaking God's own commandments. 'Please forgive me, God.' But to see Roger playing with the children! It was nice also to have Paul around, although he was still sleeping at Mary and Bill's until we could rearrange the rooms. They were very big rooms, and we soon sorted things out and Paul was back with us. It was Christmas.

The girls went to Sunday school in the hall belonging to St. Mary's, and Paul went to church. He was taking confirmation classes, which he passed and was confirmed by the Bishop of Exeter. I soon became with child, and Roger asked me to change my surname by deed poll, so that the baby would have his name, which I did, as he cared for us so much. Roger would have Rosie on his knee. He taught her the times tables, from two times, right up to twelve times, before she went to school. I taught her to read and write. I know the teachers don't like this, but if the child is willing, I think it is right. You should give them a head start. It takes all the worry out of school, and this enables the child to learn with confidence.

Rosie started school at Easter. She loved it. Every day, I would walk up to school with her and Lydia, because they had to cross the main road. I would do this four times every day. We would go on a picnic most weekends to Coypool. There was a little sand there and the River Plym where they could swim. They loved it. In the evening we would play cards, Ludo, checkers, and different board games, but mostly crib. We also played a card game where you had to see how many times you could make fifteen out of the cards you were dealt with. The children really enjoyed it. We seemed to be one happy family. But now and again Roger would lose his temper, which appeared to be over nothing. I questioned Roger about it. He said, 'I know it might sound silly, but for the first time in my life I feel so happy, here with the children and you, and my own child on the way. I get this fear in my gut that it is not going to last.' 'Roger we all get these feelings, try and keep calm and don't rock the boat, and you will have nothing to worry about.'

29

I had another very premature baby, born the 1st of August 1967. His weight was just about four pounds. We called him Robin Ivor. He cried persistently, day and night. Rosie was a sickly child, but very rarely cried. She was such a happy baby, but you never get two alike. Night after night, I walked the floor, with Robin only sleeping when Robin did. I thought I would go mad. I gave him gripe water, thinking it might be colic! I tried wrapping him snugly in a blanket, all the things I could think of, that might soothe him. I told Roger he could be in pain. As you know I had thought it was colic at first, but I don't think it was that, because sometimes if they are premature babies, things are not always developed completely. So, I took him to the doctor. He gave him a good examination. 'Other than colic, I can't think of anything else. Try adding the gripe water in with his feed. He has put on weight,' was his response.

I told Roger what the doctor said. He still cried night after night. I watched him carefully. Robin was definitely in pain. What was it? Then one night, I was walking the floor with him and I saw his little fist rub his ear. I had seen this before when one of the other children was ill. Which one? I was so tired; I couldn't think straight. Paul was over twelve years older than Robin, which is why I didn't twig. It was Paul. As you know, Paul was stone deaf in one ear because of his illness.

It was Christmas morning and it looked as if Robin had bronchitis, so I called in the doctor. It was bronchitis! 'Please doctor, will you look in his ears?' I asked. 'There is no need to, they don't get ear infections when they are this young.' 'Please! I beg you doctor.' The doctor looked at me, then he turned to examine Robin's ears. 'How did you know?' he asked, surprised. 'He has got a bad infection in his ears!' 'Because my son Paul suffered the same and ended up stone deaf in one ear,' I replied. As soon as Robin started on the medicine, we had the first good night's sleep since he was born. I was spoilt. The next day I was not allowed to lift a finger other than to see to Robin. He was so very poorly, dear little mite, but it was lovely to see him sleep peacefully for a while.

Although Robin started to sleep better, he still suffered from ear infections. Very often I was back and forwards to the doctors. We had Robin christened at St Mary's. Mary and Bill were his God Parents. They were thrilled. The other three children had been christened at St Michael's in Teignmouth. I was a little sad that day, that Mum and my stepfather weren't there as they had been for the others. I haven't written to my mum since that day, but I sent cards and flowers for her birthday and Christmas. Despite all she had done, I will still always love her.

We just had some good news. They were going to demolish this row of houses, to widen the road and make a roundabout. And we were going to be rehoused a little way up the hill from here.

We moved onto the Efford Estate in February 1968. It was a three-bedroom house. It was lovely to have a house again and a front and back garden. I could grow my own veggies and fruit again, and plenty of flowers. We had a big kitchen, plus dining room and lounge, and two toilets, one up and one down, as well as a bathroom! We could not have asked for more. Lydia and Rosie settled in their new school and they quickly made friends. Their friends were soon calling around for the girls to go out to play. Another good thing was that there was a little park at the bottom of the back garden. Roger soon knocked up a gate so that they could go in and out. Lydia loved the swings. She sat there, like a little lady, not a hair out of place, but Rosie? Well! She would shimmy up the bars, then hang upside down, no hands, just hanging on by her legs, shall I go on? I told her off time and time again, but to no avail. I had to smile to myself. It was exactly what I did at her age, and I am still here to tell the tale! If there was a tree to climb, she was up it. Talk about like-father-like-son, this was like-daughter-like-mother! She was so sure footed. Yes, now I am older I can see fear. How stupid I was. If she couldn't do it there, she would have found somewhere else to do it. At least I could keep an eye on her!

I still had a long hard fight to save Robin's hearing. Each time I saw the doctor, he told me Robin would grow out of it by the time he was seven. I knew he was wrong, but he wouldn't refer Robin to a specialist. It was heart rending to see him suffer so, and to top it all off, he also had impaired eyesight.

99

It was Christmas 1968. I had had a hysterectomy just before Christmas and came out of hospital on Christmas day. But we had a lovely Christmas, and Roger was like a big kid himself, like a dog with two tails. He had to be in on everything, from buying and wrapping the presents, to going out to the hedgerows to cut holly, and putting it all around the house. Roger made our paper chains with the children which fell down halfway through the Christmas! It was lovely.

30

In 1969, Lydia failed her eleven plus. I was not surprised. She was not willing to learn like the others had, so I never pushed her. That would have been wrong at the time. In 1970, my stepfather Roy died. That didn't surprise me either, as even when I had been up there in 1966, he was already not well. I learned more about when he was ill in hospital. It turned out Roy had cancer of the lung. They operated and took away half his lungs. No way should Mum have made Roy go back to such heavy work as making breeze blocks, with all the cement dust. On top of that, Roy also had to go to work on Saturdays, to do gardening in all winds and weather. I had said I was sorry that Mum was doing it to him, but Roy had simply said it was not as bad as what she was doing to me and the children.

Robin, on his third birthday in 1970, had to go into hospital, to have an operation on his eye, to straighten it. The doctor could see his left eye needed attention, but would he listen to me about his ears? No! He would grow out of it by the time he was seven! But the doctor must have been fed up with me, as Robin would have an ear infection every couple of months, and the doctor still wouldn't do anything about it. I think I spent more time in waiting rooms, what with his ears and patches over his right eye to make the lazy left eye work, than I did at home.

One day, I was putting in a new fuse into a plug. Robin, now in his third year, asked me what I was doing. 'Mending a fuse, my love. They get hot now and again and blow, so Mummy needs to put a new fuse in. This is a 13 amp, but they can be as little as 5 amps, depending on the power it needs,' I explained. 'Can I have a go?' he asked. 'If you want to! The red wire goes in that hole and the black in that hole, and the green one up there. Let Mummy check it now. Oh, that's lovely!' I needed to tighten the screws a bit more but, other than that, it was alright. After that, Robin came up for a cuddle. 'Mummy, I am not going to be as clever as Paul and the girls!' I said, 'Why not?' 'Because I am ill so much.' I looked at him. He wasn't as robust as the other three. I had taught Paul and Rosie to read at the age of three.

Lydia a little later, and she could read a little by the time she went to school. She could count to a hundred and do most of her letters.

I said, 'You are only three! But if you want to learn like the others, you have got to want to do it, Robin! It is not easy.' Robin said, 'But I want to learn, Mummy!' 'You have got Lydia and Rosie to help you as well! I said. So, between us, we helped him. You could see he was not hearing well, with 'stairs' coming out as 'dairs'. The girls were better than me. Although I had to teach the girls first to show them how to make 'st' sounds, and how they had to roll their tongue with some of the words. We had to check him every time he pronounced a word wrong. That is the only way we could help Robin. I soon got him reading, and the girls took over when I didn't have the time. Robin was very happy he could read now. I told him he had to learn how to count first, then write his letters A.B.C. and Robin soon mastered it all. Nothing was going to stop him. His learning became insatiable, with the pile of Ladybird books being the best books around at the time.

After Roy's funeral, Mum and Peggy started to come down and see us now and again. Peggy was having another baby, so when she came down to see me, she asked if I had anything left over from Robin's baby things. I did. I had plenty of nappies, some were still new and I told her that I was going to take them and all the baby things into town to sell them as I could do with the money, the way my children were growing out of things. But I told her that if she needed them more, I would give them to her and the cot as well, as I was putting Robin into a bed. But I still needed to order bunk beds. Peggy said she would have it all and would arrange to have the clothes and cot picked up later.

Mum was the next one to come down. Roger would always do her a few roll-ups (fags) and then, off he would go to see a mate, as he had been off sick, with TB. for quite a while. Even so, I couldn't get him to give up smoking. He did try at one time, but he was far too grumpy, so he just cut back. 'Why doesn't Roger say goodbye to me? Mum asked. 'Mum, Roger be will back soon. He has only gone over to see a mate. When the children come home from school, we will all have something to eat together, and Paul will look after the young ones. We will see you off on your train, as we always do, then we will say goodbye.'

Mum was not very happy with Peggy as she had lost the baby because she was moving a large wardrobe, still full of clothes. 'I don't think she wanted that baby,' Mum said. Peggy wrote that she had lost the baby, but asked if she could keep the baby things, as there was a very poor lady down the road. Could she have them for her? I was always ready to help anyone worse off than myself. I know life was a struggle at times, and this was one for me. I could have done with the money the clothes would have fetched from the dealers, but the dealer would have had the best of deal. So, I considered giving it all to the poor lady down the road. It was one big con on Peggy's part. (As you will see when you read on!)

Robin was doing well with his reading. Rosie said, 'Can I see if he can join the good reader's circle up the library?' 'Do you think Robin is ready for it, Rosie?' 'Yes, Mum!' was her reply. The good reader's circle is where you would read a book, and the librarian would ask questions on it, and you would get points. How many depended on how hard the book was. When they had so many points, they would get a shield. At that time, Robin was the youngest child to have been awarded a shield. And it was thanks to Rosie.

On nice days, we would go down the creek or to the Hoe for a swim, but if it was chilly, we would wander up by Plym Bridge. It was a pretty place. If you sat on the banks you might be lucky to see kingfishers, jays, squirrels, rabbits, and all kind of trees and wildflowers. There was so much beauty around. Roger would play bat and ball with the children. How different from my life with Sid, who never had time for his children. He would just sit in the chair and read, and not bother to speak to any of us at times, except to shout at the children if he thought they made too much noise. He would bellow out, 'Shut up! I came home for peace and quiet!' One day I had said, 'You have come to the wrong place, haven't you!' Paul and Lydia were such quiet children, you would only hear them now and again with a little laugh or a giggle. I wonder what he would have said if he had come home when Rosie was there. She sounded like a herd of elephants going through the house!

I saw Peggy now and again. She would bring her daughter, Dora, down for the day. Roger was back at work again. The children were all growing up, so Peggy always had a pile of clothes that the children had grown out of. She always especially took the clothes of Robin's for the poor lady down the road. Mum came down to Plymouth, but I had to meet her in town with Robin, all because she took the hump because Roger wouldn't say cheerio when he went over to see his mates. How stupid can you get!

Mum asked me if I had given Peggy the lovely lilac coat and hat set that we bought between us for one of Lydia's birthdays. 'Yes, Rosie grew out of it, so I passed it on for Dora.' 'Well, Dora never had it. I saw it in the second-hand shop! Peggy sold it the day after she visited you with all the other clothes. So, don't give her any more. You need the money, not her. She only has one child, you've got four.' I wanted to say, 'Mum! You have a short memory!' as I remembered how Mum was going to rob me blind and take all my money when I was up there in 1966. It was time I got home. Robin was not at all well and Roger was wild with me. 'If your Mum can't come out here, you're not going into town to see her.' He was right. It was nothing but a lot of silliness. I wrote and told Mum that Roger said she would be welcome here any time, but I didn't see her for a while.

Next time I saw Peggy, she asked if I would clean a house in Plymouth for her boss. I agreed so long as I could take Robin with me. Off I go. It took me a while to clean the house as it was big and very dirty, having been let out to students. When Peggy's boss came down, she paid me for all the hours I worked and was very pleased with what I had done. She asked me if I would work for her until she sold the place. I said yes. I worked for four mornings a week. I was able to take Robin with me and he would sit there and read. They soon sold the property and she asked if I would help her daughter pack up in the annex that day. The lady showed me what needed to be done downstairs in this annex, then took me upstairs. In the cot sat a little boy, a year or so younger than Robin. I couldn't help saying, 'That is like a suit I had for Robin!' 'Oh yes, I bought it all off your sister Peggy!' said Peggy's old boss, 'with a lot of other lovely things, beautiful, hand knitted clothes and a cot and other things. Nearly a complete layette. I bought it all off Peggy.' This is all that Peggy

104

scrounged, off me. She had sold it to this rich lady, instead of giving it to some very poor lady down the road. It is hard to believe that a sister could do this to me, when I could have done with the money myself. She most likely spent it on bingo, while we were going through a hard time of it. Peggy had her husband's pay. She worked part time herself. Mum looked after Dora. She had Dora's family allowance. It was more money than I had coming in at that time, when Roger was on the sick, plus we had to find the money for his medication which we had to buy at that time. I took in knitting and sewing and grew as much veg as I could.

31

It was now 1972, and Robin was off to school. Because of his problems, they wanted to put him in a 'backward school'; this is what it was called at that time. I wasn't going to have it. He was not backward. I fought for him to go into mainstream school, and I won. The lovely teacher in the baby class wanted to talk with me. She said he was a very bright child and asked if I had been teaching him. 'Yes,' I said. 'Myself and his two sisters. But you try and stop him learning! He wants a book on electronics and a soldering iron kit now. My stumbling block is the doctor, as he said he will grow out of his hearing problems by the time he is seven, but I think by the time he is seven he could be deaf.' 'I agree with you,' said the teacher.

I could have wrapped my arms around her, and I wept with sheer joy. She was going to help me to try and save Robin's hearing. The following week we were sent to Seven Trees Clinic. The doctor there was brilliant. After the hearing test he was put on the list to have his tonsils and adenoids removed. This was done within six weeks. We went back again to Seven Trees for another hearing test. The doctor was not satisfied. We had to go back to the hospital for deep cleaning. When I got there, Robin would not leave me. The nurse said parents were not allowed in while treatment was being done. But in this case, I was allowed in because Robin was better with me there. He was allowed to sit on my lap, with his head on my chest. When they put this long hook-like needle in his ear, it was *me* that squirmed, as I whispered to him, reassuring him all the time. We went there on a regular basis. Robin would tell them, 'I can feel more down there!' 'Yes, he's right!' said the nurse, as she went in again. Plus, we were still going to the eye hospital regularly for patches over his good eye.

This went on for a very long time. Robin had another operation. I can't remember what was done this time. It was to do with his ears though. Then the last operation was to have grommets inserted. What I remembered this time was a little boy in the ward whose Gran lived two doors away from us. No one had come to visit him. Robin asked, 'Can you bath us together, Mum?' I went to nurse and told her of Robin's request. 'Yes, I will come in with you.' We let them play in the bath for a while. It was good for them to relax before their operations. They gave Robin his first jab and he started to feel sleepy. 'Go and hold my friend's hand now, Mummy. I am going to sleep for a while. He's got nobody, and I know you love me. Mum, stay with him until he goes to sleep!' I did! This little boy held on to my hand, until he dropped off.

Roger was very hurt, because Robin couldn't hear him, although he was able to hear me most of the time. But not Roger. 'There must be a reason for it, Roger. Come to Seven Trees next week and see the doctor,' I suggested. Roger came along for Robin's next appointment; Roger told the doctor what was bugging him. 'We will do a test. First let your wife speak to show her tone level.' Robin was pressing the button most of the time. The doctor turned to Roger to speak, 'Here, this is your tone level.' Robin's finger never moved once. The doctor took the needle up a little way more before Robin started pressing the button again, then the doctor showed the chart to us and explained how much Robin could hear. The doctor said, 'I am sorry to say the hearing Robin has lost, I can't bring back. It's a pity he wasn't brought to me sooner. I know your wife tried to tell your doctor, but I am sorry to say this was their belief and most times they're right. Unfortunately for your two sons, the doctors were wrong and it has done permanent damage. Roger was alright after the doctor showed him the graph.

We will go back to 1972 again. Sometimes it's better to tell the complete story. This was the year the government bought in a law, that anyone living apart from their spouses for over five years could now get a divorce. So, I went back to my solicitor. He was pleased to say I would get my divorce right away this time. I had to go to the court, mainly about the children's welfare. I went to court. I had to swear on the Bible. 'Has the father of your children kept in touch with them?' 'No! Your Honour.' Then the judge said, 'We will talk about Paul first. What are your plans for him?' 'Well, Your Honour, when Paul was seven, I was told by his headmaster that if he keeps up the good work, he will end up in university. Paul is now attending Sutton High School for Boys. He is doing very well. He sits his A levels next year and if university is what he wants, I will help him all I can to get there.' The judge said, 'Now about the two girls?' 'Well, Your Honour, the same applies. I believe girls should have the same chances as a boy, to be educated.' I was granted full custody of the children, and received maintenance until they were eighteen, unless they left school before.

Roger and I got married in July 1972. Roger was still working at this time. We had a good standard of living and were able to pay for extra lessons for Paul to do technical drawing in his last year, and to buy a typewriter, as well as a secretarial course plus shorthand for Lydia. But things didn't last long. Roger got ill with rheumatoid arthritis. The sick pay was very poor. We managed Roger's medication and put a deposit on a knitting machine. I was going to take in knitting just before Paul's maintenance was to finish in a few months' time, as well as his part of the family allowance. I couldn't go out to work because of Robin being ill. I regularly had to take him here, there and everywhere. He was missing a lot of schooling, so I needed to go up to the school and get permission to help him. I asked the head teacher if I could help him. 'Yes, so long as you learn the new methods,' came the answer. I had to sit in on the maths lessons mainly, sitting on the children's seats with my long legs under my chin, and the little girls tittering!

Everything was working out well. Robin was getting stronger, and he never looked back with his lessons, but poor Roger got so crippled with the rheumatoid arthritis he couldn't work and ended up on disability pension. He also had his medication free at this time, which was a great help to us. This was 1973. Paul left school at eighteen, but he didn't go straight to university, as I had hoped he would. He went to work as a scientist, until he was twenty-one. Then he went on to Birmingham University, which I was very pleased about. Rosie passed her eleven plus and I sent her to Southway Comprehensive School.

Roger was giving me a lot of verbal abuse now, which was not nice. I put it down to him being in a lot of pain with the rheumatoid arthritis. But it was getting worse, to the point where he was knocking me around. One of the times he really hurt me, but he seemed truly sorry about it, and begged me not to leave him. And he told me his story. He had loved his father and looked up to him, but his father had died when he was nearing his fifteenth birthday, leaving a family of five. Within a short time, his mother married a seventeen-year-old Jamaican. He turned out to be a nasty kettle of fish and wouldn't let Roger's mother feed her children. They only fed themselves, and the food was kept locked up in their bedroom, the rest of the money went on drink. So, to feed themselves and their three young sisters, Roger and his younger brother Billy went around looking for scrap metal to sell to the scrap merchants, mainly around the bomb sites. This went on for a while every day after school. One day they couldn't find any scrap. What could Roger do now? They needed money for food.

Roger said, using Billy as a look out, he climbed up onto a Church roof and took some lead off it, only a little, just enough to feed them. When the food ran out, they went back for more. Roger climbed up once more, but this time he got caught. Roger told the police of their plight, so the police and welfare went around to their house and saw that they were all suffering from malnutrition. The three young girls were put into a home right away, and Roger and Billy were locked up until they were brought to court.

Roger had a custodial sentence until he was twenty-one and was sent up country to learn a trade. But Billy was sent to borstal, where he fell in with a bad lot. After that, he was in and out of prison for the rest of his life. He was really a bad person. But Roger blamed himself for the way Billy turned out. If only he hadn't taken him that evening, he said. I don't know how to put this. Even if Billy had gone into care, like the girls, they were no angels. Shall I put it that they were a disadvantaged family to lose their father at such a tender age? This is the kindest way I can put it. They are not my story. It was only to explain a little about Roger, and what happened in my story later.

I was able to take in knitting now. I mastered the knitting machines. But I just lost something like six pounds a week, what with losing the maintenance and Paul's family allowance. That was the biggest part of my income gone. It left us very short of money. I phoned up a firm that needed knitters, and they took me on. The money was good, but it was only during the summer and winter seasons. There were quite long breaks in-between.

109

32

It was the summer of 1974. Lydia left school a month before her sixteen birthday and was able to start to work for S.W.E.B. accounts office. She had done very well at school, with eleven C.S.E. grade ones. At the time, that was equal to a grade three in O levels. I was very pleased with her. The headmaster wanted Lydia to go to high school to get her A levels. I think Lydia could have turned over to high school curriculum, though she might have needed extra lessons in math, due to being taught logarithm, and not having been taught applied and pure maths as Paul had been. But I was more worried about her welfare. If she found herself out of her depth, she would become very unhappy, and could be out of her comfort zone. So, when I went up to see the headmaster and Lydia's teacher, and told them my fears and her teacher fully agreed with me. 'I would suggest evening classes,' said her teacher. 'Yes, I agree with that!' I said, 'and maybe Lydia can achieve her A level maths.' I think the headmaster was a little disappointed. When she was settled in her place of work and was going to evening classes she met a very nice boy called Keith from a very nice family. Keith's dad would come and pick Lydia up and take them on to a function. Sometimes he would come and sit with Roger and myself and we would have a cup of tea and a good old chat, then he would pick Lydia and Keith up. He even brought Lydia home. This went on for a while. We seemed happy enough. Roger would blow up and get violent now and again, but it was not every day. Sometimes it could be six months or more, with him being very grumpy as he was in so much pain. Most evenings though, he would be in bed by nine o'clock as he had taken his sleeping tablets.

It was coming up to the end of 1975. Keith went to university, and Lydia and Keith parted company. Keith's dad said, 'I didn't want this to happen. We loved Lydia, but I think their decision was right, and I said so too.' Lydia carried on with her evening classes. We were now in 1976, with April approaching, and Paul's twenty-first birthday. We pulled out all the stops and gave him a party and a gold signet ring which took all our savings again. Paul was at University now.

Lydia had met a new boyfriend, but she seemed to change towards me. We only took a very small keep from her. She had most of her wages. I didn't believe in fleecing your children. I did all her washing and ironing, her meals were on the table when she got home from work, and she never believed in washing her dishes after her. Lydia got paid monthly. Then one day I asked her if she could pay me right away as I needed to get some bread and milk for the morning before the shop closed. Lydia turned to me and said, 'You will wait until I am ready to give it to you, and not before.'

Lydia gave it to me after eight, but by then it was a bit late for the shops. I said, 'Thanks a bunch!' I was cross with her. She went out with her new boyfriend. I could see Lydia was changing towards me. I felt she wasn't the loving child I once knew. One day she came home from work, and I had not had time to doing the ironing. I had planned to do it that evening. Lydia wanted a blouse that was in the wash that day. As she was getting the ironing board out, banging and slamming everything, next there was an almighty bang. She had blown the iron up. She ran screaming from the room. Next, she was going out the door.

The next thing Lydia said was, 'I am bringing Jake around to meet you both on Friday.' It was early August 1973. Roger said it sounded like they were thinking about getting married. Roger found out about the reception. It would be about £40, a lot of money in those days. I would be making the cake, but I needed to pay to have it iced. I bought the pattern for the dresses, and I priced up all the materials, then the taxis on top. It would have taken us about six months to pay for it all, with a bit of luck. But don't forget Roger was on the sick, and I could only do part time work, because of Robin. I was still taking him to all the appointments that I have written about.

On this particular Friday, I cooked some sausage rolls and made some sandwiches, and in they both came. We shook hands, and I made tea and coffee, and we sat around the dining room table. I said, 'Come on, what do you want and tell us?' I thought they were going to say they were getting engaged. Jake did all the talking. 'We want to get married in three weeks' time, when Lydia's eighteen.' 'Can't you get engaged first?' I asked. 'No! That's a waste of money,' he said. 'It will take us a while to make the dresses, for Lydia, Rosie and myself,'

I said. 'She is not getting married in white,' Jake said. I replied, 'You have got to book the Church, they will have got a waiting list.' 'I'm an atheist so, there will be no church wedding.' 'It was everything as he wanted.

Roger got hold of this little *bumpish* git by his shirt collar, and marched him through the passage, opened the front door, and said, as he let go the collar, 'Don't you ever darken our doorstep again!' After we heard Lydia follow him out the front door, Roger put his arms around me and, in between sobs, cried, 'I won't be able to walk that pretty little girl down the aisle, will I, Faith?'

When Lydia came home that evening, she was full of herself. 'Will you sign this paper for me?' There was no, *please Mum*. 'Who's paying for the wedding? I asked, and received a sharp answer from Lydia, 'His parents!' 'What does Jake work at?' 'He hasn't got a job.' She was snappy with every answer she gave me; it was so hurtful. I told her, 'By the way, we won't be coming to the wedding.' I didn't want to be near her with that attitude, and I added, 'We can't afford it,' which was true. 'You know Roger and I've only got work clothes; all our money went on you children. What's this paper you want me to sign?' 'Your permission for me to get married.' 'But you don't need that. You're eighteen at the end the month.' 'I need your permission for the bans to be read, three weeks before I am eighteen.' 'So, I am good for something, I see!' as I signed it. I did what a mother should do right up to the end. I washed and set her hair that day and waved her goodbye. I never said a bad word to her, but my heart was breaking. What did I do so wrong that she turned against me like that? But I knew it was the boyfriend.

We didn't see Lydia for the next few years. A part of me did want to see her again, and a part of me didn't. Roger was getting more violent towards me. Mum came down to see me once more before she died in February 1977. I could never hate my Mum, in fact I still loved her. It was Mum doing what she thought was right, but it is life itself that is a bitch and had made a hard woman of her. I was determined this wasn't going to happen to me. I had to stay soft and tender, like my Gran taught me. Just be kind to everyone. Her motto was to treat everyone as you would like them to treat you.

33

Then I went to Mum's funeral and back home the same day. Shortly after, Colin came to see me. 'Faith, you never had anything of Mum's!' 'I don't want anything Colin.' 'But Faith, you did so much for Mum. We all knew you gave money to her while our stepfather was in hospital.' I was thinking of something they would say no to, as I thought that if Mum had wanted me to have something, she would have given it to me when she gave something to Rosie and Robin the last time we last saw her. So, I said 'Mum's engagement ring.' 'That's O.K. by me,' said Colin, 'I will see what Peggy and Theo and April think.' I had a letter from Colin to say that *the ring was mine* which surprised me. 'Peggy will bring it down next time she comes.' Peggy came down shortly after, and gave me a ring, but it was not Mum's ring! This was a cheap and nasty ring. The stones looked like just glass with claws. In Mum's ring the stones were not set in claws. Someone had swapped it. I threw it in a drawer.

Roger was very violent now, but it was classed as domestic violence and I got no help at all. Then he went quiet for a while but was very moody and harder to get on with; not the nice person I knew at first, when he couldn't do enough to help me. Roger had been to see his sister. She told him that Billy had been stabbed and died in prison. I could see something was wrong; he was like a caged animal when he came home. I knew he was ready to blow his top, so I got the children to their bedrooms, and went into the bedroom to see if he needed anything to eat and drink.

The next minute, he was off the bed with his hand around my throat. He was trying to open the bedroom window with the other, and he tried to throw me out. Roger had this cold stare in his eyes, shouting at me, 'It's all your fault! Billy is dead. Are you satisfied now?' I wondered where he got the strength from, as he was riddled with rheumatoid arthritis. Some days he could hardly move and yet now he was trying to throw me like I was a rag doll. I don't think I will ever forget that cold look in his eyes and the look of hatred on his face.

I managed to get away and call the police, but sadly they couldn't do anything as it was domestic violence. That is, until Roger punched one of the policemen. He was taken off to the police cells, to come up before the judge. The police came back and asked if I had anywhere to go. I said I didn't, and he gave me the address for a battered wives' home. I made the policeman a cup of tea. We talked about the law. 'We see some awful things sometimes,' the policeman said, 'and we can't do a thing about it.' 'I expect he's got to kill me before you can?' The police shrugged his shoulders. I packed a few things and off we went to this battered wives' home. It was awful there. It was bedlam, with children just running amok. You couldn't put anything down. They just took the food off your plate. Nothing was safe.

The children said, 'Mum this is worse than being home.' 'Let's stick it out until you break up for your summer holidays, and I will see if we can go up and stay with Aunty Peggy, is that alright?' 'Yes Mum!' I needed to see about a divorce and the D.H.S.S. as I had no money before leaving Plymouth. We went to stay with Peggy for a few days. I think it was something to do with the Queen's Coronation. I would think it was her Silver Jubilee. Then we made tracks for home, to find no Roger there, only a letter, saying that the judge had sent him to a custodian hostel for a psychiatric assessment. Next, I had a letter from the psychiatrist, asking if I would see him.

When I got there at the arranged time, the psychiatrist came to greet me. 'I am pleased you have come along, because I am getting nowhere with your husband's assessment, I hope you can help me!' 'How can I help you? I asked. 'By telling me all you know?' I told him what Roger and his sister Beryl had told me about the early days, and I told him of our married life and how this lovely man had turned into a monster. 'I felt the last time we were together, I wasn't the person he was talking to!' 'Yes! That's it!' said the psychiatrist, 'You have cleared the mystery. Each trauma he had, damaged him. I am afraid he is suffering from schizophrenia. In his outbursts, you became his mother. Has he ever hit the children?' 'Not to my knowledge.' The psychiatrist went on to say, 'We can control these outbursts with tablets.' 'I am not willing to try! I am going to divorce him.'

I asked Rosie and Robin if we should move from here and put into a mutual exchange of houses. They both agreed. Roger was forever at me to take him back. He was very persistent. He got on to me again. This time he was looking very ill. I started to think how he had helped me in the beginning, and how he had kept all his promises about my children's education. They had everything they needed for their education, plus food and clothes and a nice home. Paul had extra classes on technical drawing and all the instruments he needed. Lydia wanted typing classes. We had bought her a typewriter, so she could do her work at home. Roger went without, to provide some of these things. He had been very keen for them to learn.

How could I turn my back on him now? We all agreed that as long as he took the tablets for schizophrenia, he could come back. It was Easter 1978. Paul was home from university, so he could help me with the move, and we moved to Austin Farm Estate. Paul went back to university, Rosie and Robin went back to school. We all settled in our new home. It was a little smaller, but still had three bedrooms, a big kitchen and a large living area, a storeroom, and a front and back garden.

Roger was very moody, but that was to be expected, as he was in so much pain. Roger took very strong sleeping tablets every evening so he could get to sleep. He was always in bed by nine. This gave me a good opportunity, on Fridays, to keep my promise I made to the children. In order to have a good discussion about everything that had occurred in the week, we kept the T.V. on low. We made all the decisions together. I felt they had the right to do this. If we disagreed on a subject, we would talk it out, until we are all satisfied.

34

It was now August 1978. The children and I went to a wedding. It was my brother Colin's and Daphne's youngest daughter's wedding. We didn't want it to end. We had a lovely day out with the family. It was lovely to laugh and feel free. But all too soon it was time to make tracks for home. We were not too badly off now as my knitting had really taken off, and I became one of her top knitters. I was knitting the sample and helping her to make sure the patterns were correct for the other knitters. My knitting went to many countries, and I was on a good wage. But it was not to last. She went bankrupt, so once again, I was left without a job.

It was now April 1979. I was in the kitchen when something was telling me to go to my brother Colin. I hadn't seen or heard from him since his daughter's wedding. The feeling was very strong. I said to Roger that I needed to hitch-hike to Torquay. He asked me why, 'Because I know my brother needs me!' Roger said, 'You have got one of your feelings again?' 'Yes,' I said. 'Well, we can take the rent money for now.' So, I wrote to Daphne and Aunt Paula. Why Aunt Paula? Because Colin was her favourite in the family. We set the date for Wednesday the 11th of April 1979. Roger and I caught the train to Newton Abbot and took a taxi up to Aunt Paula, then off to Colin's.

When, Daphne opened the door, her face told me all that I feared. Colin was upstairs. She couldn't get me there fast enough. 'He has been praying you would come.' When I got in the bedroom, I couldn't believe my eyes. This man, my brother, was six foot two inches tall in his stocking feet, with very broad shoulders. About sixteen stone when I last saw him, now he was laid in his bed, and he was nothing but a bag of bones. I was fighting back the tears as I bent down to kiss him. 'Oh, Faith. I needed to see you so badly, I knew you would come if I prayed. Faith, I am dying.' 'Don't say silly things like that, Colin.' Still trying to fight the tears back, it was so painful watching him. This was the brother I loved so much, who had always stood by me when we were young.

'So, what do you want, Colin?' 'When the time comes, for you to look after Daphne. I am so worried about her. You're the only one I can trust to help her. Promise me, Faith, that you will do what you can.' 'I promise my upmost.' 'That's good enough for me. I know you will give your all.' We talked a little more. 'I've got a surprise for you,' I said. I went downstairs and sent Aunt Paula up, made a nod to Roger to go up with her, as she would be shocked at what she saw. Roger followed Aunt Paula up. I had a cup of tea with Daphne, trying not to break down.

I asked how the girls were, and we talked about our children and other small talk. Soon Roger and Aunt Paula came down saying that Colin would like to see me again. I went up. 'Did you like your surprise?' 'Yes, it was nice to see the Old Gal. She is looking good for her age!' 'Aunt Paula always loved you best, Colin! She told me that back in 1955, just before you got married to Daphne. That's why I thought you both would like to see each other!' 'Trust you, Faith! You're always thinking of others!' We talked a little about the good old days. 'Well, I must go now, Colin. But don't you worry. I won't let you down.' 'I know you won't.' 'I love you,' I said, and kissed my Colin goodbye, knowing this would be our last kiss.

It was time for us to go. 'I am leaving you next door's phone number, Daphne. Phone me if you need me.' Daphne arranged for her brother, Dan, to take us to Newton Abbot. I gave Daphne a big hug and kiss. We got in Dan's car. As I waved goodbye to Daphne, the tears started to roll down my cheeks. Aunt Paula was sitting in front with Dan. She turned to me and said, 'How did you know, Faith?' I couldn't answer her, so Roger did. 'She just had one of the feelings she gets. I have found she is never wrong when she gets them.' 'I agree she was always the sensitive one of the family,' said Aunt Paula. 'Even when she ran away from my Mum, her Gran, we never knew how she found my place. She was so young.' Roger said, 'She had someone with her! Now I believe her, after this situation with her brother.' We dropped Aunt Paula off. As she went, she thanked us for thinking of her. 'I appreciate you both,' were her parting words.

Dan dropped us at Newton Abbot station. I pulled myself together. Roger and I got on the train for Plymouth. Two days after, on Friday the 13th of April 1979, my Colin died. This was a very sad loss for me, because of the bond we had shared from childhood. There was only me and my sister April left now. Roger and I went to the funeral, but Roger had to take me out. I just went to pieces. Georgie Scown came up to us. He was one of the Funeral Directors, and a cousin to Colin and me. I said, 'Georgie, Colin was only forty-nine, he was a good brother to me, he helped me through some tough times in my life. He was always there for me.' Georgie had also been a mate to Colin, before he went into army. Roger stepped back, as Georgie put his arm around me. 'Faith, I know how close you and Colin were.' Georgie touched his heart, 'Keep him close here, and talk about him as if he is still here with you, and Colin will never die.' Georgie gave me a hug.

I will never forget the way Georgie helped me to face that day. and the rest of my life; He was such a lovely man. So, I dried my tears, hid my broken heart over Colin, and got on with what Colin had asked of me. The first problem I had was Daphne. She didn't want anyone in the cottage. I got the two daughters, Pat and Sarah, to put their Mum to bed, as she had already been drinking, so that she could sleep it off. I was there to welcome the people back for food and drink. This is what Colin would expect of me.

35

Then my Dad started. He wanted Colin's medals. Colin had been in the army and fought in a lot of conflicts and was a long serving soldier. I didn't think much of my Dad. Why? Because of what my Mum had told me. Colin had won a lot of medals, plus the long service medal. It was his wife Daphne who had stayed home, wondering if her husband was going to come home alive or maimed, and there was Dad, shouting and demanding to see Daphne, to get the medals. I said quietly to Dad, 'Daphne is indisposed. She has just lost her husband. Show a little bit of respect. And Colin's medals belong to Daphne and their two daughters. Dad said, 'No, they belong me. I am his father.' Right or wrong, he was rubbing me up the wrong way. I could not stop myself. 'What Father! You were never there when we needed you; when as children we were sometimes starving.' 'Faith you have a sharp tongue like your Mother.'

'Dad, you can't say that. You don't even know me. I am nothing like Mum. I am gentle and kind, and I love my brothers and sisters, and I will fight their battles for them, when they can't. So, Dad, you are out of order, so sit down,' and, pointing at the door, 'or there's the door.' 'Please yourself. But they are not your medals.' By this time Dan, Daphne's brother, had come in. 'What is the fuss about?' 'Nothing. Faith's taken care of it,' said a voice. All I wanted to do was to go into a corner and cry, but I had to stay strong, as this is what Colin had asked of me on his death bed, '*I trust you to take care of my Daphne,*' as he knew she would be wrapped up in her own grief.

The girls had just finished clearing up. 'I am staying with your Mother for a while.' 'Thanks Aunty,' they said. 'Please don't let anyone take your Father's medals,' I told them. 'They belong to your part of the family. Please tell your Mother not to give them to my Dad, I beg you. When he is hard up, he will sell them. That's how much they meant to him.' I told Roger I had to stay. 'You can see the state she's in.' 'Yes, Faith.' 'Roger, ask Pauline if the children can phone now and again.' This had been put in place with Pauline and the children before I left Plymouth, as I needed to know my children were safe.

I was there for about two weeks. Daphne's mum came to see her, and I told her I was going home. 'No, you can't!' her mum said. 'You are doing such a good job here, looking after Daphne.' 'It's your place to look after your daughter, not mine,' I said. 'I have got a young family of my own to look after. I need to go home. I have done more than Colin would have expected. He wouldn't want me to desert my children and babysit his wife for the rest of her life. It is your place to see to her. She needs medical help for her drinking problem.' That day I went home. Dan drove me to the station and told me he had heard I left his Mum with a flea in her ear. 'Yes, Dan, but I've got a young family at home,' 'I know Faith. You've done more than your fair share. A big thanks from me and my family. We've got to take over now!'

There was a lovely welcome home; my children's smiling faces and their arms going around my neck with hugs and kisses all round. We had missed each other so much. When I got back, we carried on our Friday night discussions, as before. We needed to, as Rosie was now seventeen. Roger started to come down hard on Rosie. She was not allowed out with her friends at the weekends or evenings. This was going over the top, so I tried to talk to Roger. 'She has got to have a little bit of freedom, Roger.' 'And what happened to Lydia when she turned seventeen?' Roger asked, 'she met up with that awful chap, and left when she was eighteen, and we have not seen her since. You can't tell me you weren't heartbroken.' 'But it was *her* choice, you can't live their life for them!' 'And look what happened to my own young sisters,' Roger said. 'They all ended up bad.' Then he just clammed up and wouldn't say any more.

The following Friday, I told Rosie and Robin what had happened. 'Have you got any ideas? Think for a minute, something might come to you.' 'No, Mum.' 'I was hoping you would. I have got an idea. I don't like it because two wrongs don't make a right, but we can't rock the boat. But this calls for desperate measures. I am going to have to lie for you, Rosie. If I push Roger too far, he might turn violent again, and we don't want that do we?' 'No, Mum!' 'So, I don't want you two to tell lies, you promise me?' 'Yes, Mum.' All the time

120

I was praying to God, to forgive me. I didn't like what I was about to do.

'Well Rosie, you are a prefect now. You have done the odd duty at school and you were allowed to stay late at school. Going into your last year, you are being asked to do more extra duties. Get the gist?' 'Yes, Mum.' 'What do you think?' 'Good, Mum.' 'I will cover for you, but I don't like telling lies, so don't abuse it. But you must have a normal life and some freedom. Now Rosie, I know you don't want to go to university, and there has been a reason I made you stay at school, hoping you will get at least one A level, so you can get a job away from home. It's only next year, so you need to apply soon. What do you think of that place where Paul worked as a scientist? It is good pay, plus it's got a hostel.' 'I will apply, Mum.' 'The last thing I want, is for you to leave me. But it the only way for you to have freedom, with friends and a normal life, but I hope you will come home to see Robin and me. We love you and this is how we will have to handle it.'

Peggy came down to see me shortly after I came home, to gloat. She hardly had a foot inside the door before she started to tell me, 'I went to the spiritualist church the other evening, and the medium came over and told me, '*Your Mother wants to speak to you. You are the daughter that is wearing her engagement ring.*' I can't remember what else was said. I knew it was all lies and I wasn't interested in what she had to say, as Peggy had only came to rub my nose in it now that Colin was dead. I played along with Peggy, 'But I thought Colin said I was to have the ring, and all the family agreed.' 'All but me,' said Peggy, 'so I gave you my old one.' 'I knew that it was not Mum's ring right away. I didn't want anything from Mum. I told Colin, but he insisted. But what a difference in principal, between brother and sister. It doesn't say much about you though, Peggy.' This kind of wiped the smirk off her face. 'Who's got the ring? You or Dora?' I asked. 'I sold it when I was hard up.' 'So, that is how much the ring meant to you? You sold everything, including all the clothes you conned out of me, for that poor lady down the road. And there was no poor lady down the road, it was your rich boss. I know you had good money for the clothes because she told me.'

36

Rosie left school at eighteen, in 1980, and went away to work as a scientist. With day release, she worked her way up to become a science officer and was soon running her own department, and this is where she met her husband-to-be. Now there was only Robin left. Paul came home from university during his breaks and when he finished university in 1981. But he was in no hurry to get a job. I felt Roger was going to be violent to Paul, as Roger said to me, 'I will kick his teeth in if he doesn't get a job soon.' I don't think Roger was taking his tablets. So, when a letter came for Paul about a job, I encouraged him to take it. But I must have handled it badly. He went away thinking I didn't want or love him anymore, and I didn't see him for a while. But I was right. Roger was not taking his tablets.

Roger started to pick on Robin next, but Robin could not take any more, and he asked me to take him away. What else could I do; we had given Roger so many chances. I asked Roger outright if he was taking his tablets. When he said no, I told him that we would have to leave, as I would not let Robin be a victim of his violent ways. Roger said, 'Take Robin, and go!' So, I went up to Peggy's. I got a job and a flat, ready to live in Teignmouth again. When Robin said he didn't want to live there, but wanted to go back to Plymouth until he finished at his old school, which was over three years away, we set off, back to Plymouth,

I stayed with a friend, but she could only put us up for a few weeks. It was harder to get a flat in Plymouth. We walked the streets to find accommodation. We were sent here, there and everywhere. At the next place on the list, the lady said, 'This is not fit accommodation for nice people like you and your son, as most of these people have been in prison. I will give you an address. This lady will put you up. So off we went again. We found the place. It was a hotel. She took in D.H.S.S. people for the winter, and she took us in. Robin and I had to share a room, but it was better than nothing. I saw my solicitor to ask how my divorce was going. 'You should get a social worker soon. They have got to sort out Robin's interests first,' he said. I agreed that that was very important.

The social worker sent for me. Walking up the road, a weird feeling came over me, like my legs didn't want to move. Every step I took was hard; my legs were like lumps of lead. I got to the social worker's office. It was as if she was attacking me all the time with questions about why I was stopping Robin seeing his father? 'I am not. Robin is fourteen. He has got a mind of his own. I wanted to settle in Teignmouth; he didn't, so I had to come back to Plymouth,' was my answer. 'No one has approached me to see Robin, so how can I say no?' The social worker said, 'I don't believe you,' and carried on asking questions about my childhood and why I did this, and why I did that? This social worker was aggressive toward me for a full hour. She never let up once. I don't think she had read up anything about Roger. 'We will set up a meeting with his father,' she said. However, each time Robin was ill. After a while she said, 'Next time, you bring Robin, whether he is ill or not.' The next time, we were both ill. I couldn't even phone. This social worker burst into my room. She didn't even knock. She took one look at us, said sorry and left.

I think it was the damp basement room, as I had a chest infection and Robin had croup. The social worker came to see us again. What a difference! She said sorry. I said, 'Would you like to speak to Robin on your own?' 'Yes, please,' the social worker said, 'do you mind?' I asked her how long for and she said about a quarter of an hour. 'I will make us a cup of tea in the kitchen, then I will be back,' I said. When I returned, she said, 'I believed what your husband told me, that you were a bad mother, that you kept the children up on a Friday evening to watch horror films! 'Well, Roger was telling the truth there! We led him to believe it! We had the film on very low in the background, just in case Roger woke up and came down. But it is better if you ask Robin what we were doing,' I said. The social worker turned to Robin. And Robin said, 'When Mum took Dad back, because he was ill, Rosie and I were very nervous. Every Friday we would have a discussion on anything and everything that might be worrying us. Then Rosie left home, and Dad kept on at me. I couldn't seem to do anything right in his eyes. Then one Friday I asked Mum to take me away, and she did.' I said, 'What Robin said is correct. Does this make me a bad Mum? I thought Friday was the best evening, as they had all weekend to do their homework.'

123

I found Lydia again, and I asked if she would just let Robin sleep in her spare room until we got the house back, as the basement we were sleeping in was so damp. I was worried about Robin's health, as he was a very weak child, but the answer came back no. Rosie and David came down to see us, staying at the hotel a couple of times. Every time, they wanted us to go back and live with them, but Robin wanted to stay at his school. He was happy there, but Rosie and David were worried about us, I think. But then my Rosie was always there for me, and up until this day she is still there for me.

The divorce went through. I got full custody of Robin, and we moved back to the house. Roger moved to a flat but carried on pestering me since he knew I was working at the hotel, cooking breakfast. I was only getting ten pounds a week, as that was all I was allowed to earn while I was on DHSS, but that ten pounds could buy Robin and me a lot of extras. It went a long way in those days, and it was well worth it.

37

One evening, Robin was doing his homework. He didn't finish until nine thirty. That was a heavy load of homework for one evening. I said, 'Robin are you ready for bed now?' 'No, Mum. I've got lines! Words I got wrong in French dictation. I have got to do over a thousand words. I told the teacher I couldn't hear her, but she didn't take any notice of me.' 'You didn't misspell it, you just didn't hear! That is two different things, Robin!' 'But I got thirty words wrong.' 'You mean thirty you didn't hear! The teachers want you to do every word a hundred times. That's three thousand words. Being your mother, I am stepping in, otherwise you will be here all night and will not be fit for school tomorrow. Do ten of each!' 'But I will get into trouble, Mum.' 'You won't. *I* will! Because it is me stopping you! It is too much. I will write a letter now for you to hand in with your homework. You've got nothing to worry about. It won't come back on you.' I had to watch his health, and I thought it was grossly unfair that he was being punished, because the teacher didn't take any notice of him when he said he could not hear. Of course, he would get them all wrong.

A few days after, I had a letter from the current head of languages. He tore strips off me, which I had expected. 'I do not like parents interfering with their child's homework. They must do lines when we give them,' he said, and invited me into school. A discussion followed. 'I am his Mother! I am sorry. I disagree with you. Robin sat down from half past five to half past nine. That's four hours on top of his schoolwork. Do you know what energy this takes out of my Robin? When my Robin is at school, he will need twice the concentration of a normal child to compensate for his loss of hearing and eyesight. Robin is willing to learn at all times. His aim is to beat his brother, who has just finished University. When he puts his hand up to say, 'Please Miss, I can't hear you,' I would expect them to take notice of him, not punish him with three thousand words as lines. If I had let Robin do the lines, he wouldn't have been fit for school the next day. As his Mother, I had to make this decision. What would you have done if it was your child?'

Then it dawned on the head of languages which Robin we were talking about. He said, 'You are the mother that kept Robin in mainstream! You were right to do so. He is a credit to the school. Your Robin is a very intelligent and well-behaved child. But I am sorry to say, he is not doing well at languages, and he will never pass his oral. I had made a note saying I wanted to see you because of Robin's deafness. I think it would be better at this stage to take him out of languages and give him two other subjects. What are his hobbies?' I said, 'electronics and geology.' 'I will have a word with the headmaster and see what we can do. Then I will have a word with Robin and see what subjects he might like to do.' I said, 'Thank you. I can't ask for more,' and left.

A couple of days later, Robin came home from school saying he had been taken out of his two language classes and had been given electronics and geology. I was so pleased for him and gave him a big hug. I had a lovely letter from the head of languages. He said he was very sorry for what happened in that class. 'We do want Robin to do well!' he said. 'He works so hard. We wish more children were like him. He is a real credit to the school.'

Roger was still bothering me nearly every day I was at work. One day he was there, and he wanted to give me some money. I said, 'You can't buy your way back. The answer is no. I don't want your money.' Roger went on to say, 'I had a very large pay-off from English China Clay. You deserve a part of that payment. I want you to have it with no strings attached.' At that moment I saw a little of the old Roger. The money would come in handy, as my Rosie was getting married, and it would help a lot. The wedding was to take place in Swansea. It was 1982, and Robin and I were going up to Swansea to meet David's parents that weekend. Jean and Joe were a lovely couple. I told them I was not in a situation to do a lot. 'But I think I will be able to do the wedding dress, and the four bridesmaids' dresses.' 'That will be a great help. We can do the rest, as you have saved us a lot of money by having the wedding up here. And we can also put you and Robin up.'

Rosie and David and Carol, one of Rosie's bridesmaids, came down for the weekend to help pick the dresses out. We went to Dingles, as there was a sale on there. It was a posh shop! We met up with Lydia, as she was maid of honour, and we all trooped into the bride's department. Rosie tried on a dress one of the others had picked out. I said no to that one. She tried on the next. It was no to that one too. Then I found it! 'This is the one! Try this one for me, please.' She came out and stood on the podium. She looked so lovely with the camelot sleeves. It was a beautiful dress. Then the salesgirl came out with a long veil to match and a tiara. They all agreed with me. It was right. She looked a picture.

I turned to hide a tear in my eye, and I noticed a tear in Lydia's eye. I wonder if it was a tear of regret, that she hadn't waited for a wedding like this herself. Next was the bridesmaids' dresses. We settled on the colour lilac. As Rosie and I were picking out dresses for the two little bridesmaids, Rosie said, 'What about juliet caps for their headdress?' 'Oh, that would be lovely,' I said, and we soon found them. Now for the two older ones. They had settled on their dresses and headdresses already. I paid for the lot. With everything done, just the hen party was left that evening.

38

I met Edwin shortly after. I was not really interested in men. Then it was time for Rosie's wedding. This was the day I had been waiting for. It was the 4th of September 1982, the same date as Lydia's wedding day six years earlier. Lydia said, 'When Rosie says her vows, I will say mine again.' I think I was right; Lydia *did* have regrets. Most of my family came, but not Peggy and Tim. It was a wonderful get together. It was a lovely wedding, and everything went off well. Jean and Joe had done us proud. In the evening, we were all dancing. When the song 'Sisters' started again, my sister April and I were out like a shot. This was our party piece. We had the floor to ourselves. What a giggle we had as we swung each other around. What happy memories it brought back. April and I felt like kids again.

But it was all over too soon. We said our goodbyes, and went home again, back to the same old thing. The next time I left work there was Roger, saying, time after time, that he would take the tablets if he could come back. I had heard that before. But he would not take no for an answer. What was I going to do? He was driving me nuts. I started seeing a bit more of Ed now and then. He brought up the question of my house. How long had I lived in council property and things like that? Then came the question, would I marry him?! I asked for time to think about it. I really didn't want to marry anyone. Robin and I were happy together. I talked to Robin about what he thought. 'He seems nice enough, Mum. I don't see why not!' I still had my doubts, but the next day there was Roger again, pleading with me to take him back. 'No,' I said. 'Look how miserable you made your own son, Robin, feel last time. I can't trust you anymore, because I don't think you will ever change, Roger.'

That evening Ed asked me to marry him and I said yes. I thought it might get Roger out of my hair. Not a good reason to get married again but I couldn't take it anymore. Sometimes the look in Roger's eyes made me scared, and he would grip my arm so I couldn't get away. With hindsight, I should have gone to the police, and Robin and I should have stayed on our own.

Ed and I got engaged on my birthday. I was forty-eight now. We were going to get married in January. But a few days before the wedding I said to Robin, 'I don't think I want to marry Ed. There is something about him. I can't put my finger on it. I am not sure, but maybe it is one of my feelings.' Robin said, 'Don't be silly, Mum. Just because you had a bad marriage with Dad, it could be you're just getting cold feet.' So, in January 1983, we were married. His two grown up children came. His daughter was just over eighteen, and his son was sixteen and a half.

Ed also had his landlady and husband as guests. I had Robin Rosie, David, Lydia and her husband, Peggy and Tim, my April and Colin's Daphne, and a few friends to join us at the house. It was an open house, with a buffet and drinks. I did not know when Ed and his two children left the reception. Everyone was shouting for Ed, but he was nowhere to been found. They had been missing for some time, when someone said he had gone for more drink, but that was hours ago. I said he hadn't told me he was going. I thought, this is a fine start to a marriage! Maybe my gut feeling was right not to marry Ed. And I was right! This was a time I didn't listen to my feelings. It turned out they had gone to the pub.

Betty, whom I got to know well later, said to Ed, 'I thought you got married today?' 'Yes!' said Ed. 'Well, where is your wife?' 'At home with the guests.' 'What! For over three hours! And you here with these two? I take it they are your children?' 'Yes,' Ed said. Betty was mad with all three of them. 'You all need a kicking up the backside, leaving that poor woman on her own all this time to see to your guests. I pity that poor woman if that's how you're going to treat her.' I think this was my worst marriage. The abuse I had to take from him. He was sly never to do this in front of people though. He always made sure he seemed to be the loving husband. Very crafty! Our marriage was not a marriage, except in name alone, as he went to bed drunk every night. This didn't worry me. I hadn't had sex for years with Roger being so ill. But I couldn't stand the smell of stale of beer. I just turned my back on him every night after that.

I was prepared to go along with things like this. He was my husband now. How could I get out of it? What he did were such petty things, that's all. I was tied to him. He was a drunkard and a gambler.

129

What had I let myself in for? Two of the things I hated most. Ed never let my Robin or the other children see how nasty he was to me. He was so careful. He wouldn't leave when I asked him to go, saying, 'Why should I? This is my home now, and you do what I say.' I tried to make a go of our marriage, if you can call it a marriage, but I was his servant, and nothing more.

I managed to stop Ed gambling by telling him that if he didn't stop, I would throw him out, or try to take it further. I didn't know if I could, but it seemed to do the trick. Then I got him off the spirits. I said we were in too much debt. It was the first time in my life I had been in debt. I said we would get thrown out of this house. So, I won another round. From now on he just drank beer, and even that I was able to control a little. I cut his spending money back to forty pounds a week. I was only getting family allowance plus my ten pounds. I was trying hard to get a job as I realized Ed had no money and was way in the red at the bank. I told Ed he needed to get a proper job as well as me. He found *me* a job first! Typical chauvinistic pig.

The job was in a pub doing lunch, serving drinks and food. I was like a fish out of water. I had been brought up when women didn't go in pubs on their own. I was shaking like a leaf. Roddy and Maggie ran the pub. I was introduced to Betty. Yes! The same Betty. She took me under her wings and showed me the ropes. I was a quick learner, and I was soon changing barrels as well. Betty loved that, as we never had to wait for Roddy to do it. Betty and I became good friends, and we always looked after each other.

Now Viv joined us. She was to make sandwiches at the bar while Betty and I served the drinks and the other meals. But Betty did not take to her. Viv was a bit loud, and she would use very choice words like, 'If you don't behave yourself, I will kick you in the b---s!' and sometimes a little more colourful. She was a character, but under it all she had a heart of gold. She said, 'Faith, you got to give them some lip! You don't have to be like me, but more like Betty.' We all got on like a house on fire. Before long, I was not that shy, timid person anymore. Between them, Betty and Viv brought me out of my shell, and I found myself fitting in.

The young and old would come to me with their troubles, in different ways. I soon had a load of pamphlets I got from various places. I would tell them I was not qualified to give them advice. I simply suggested they go to this place, or that place, and gave them a pamphlet. It worked. We three made a good team, which brought more trade. Roddie and Maggie were pleased, and so were our customers. Whatever heartache we had at home was left at the doorstep. We became actresses. We were good at our jobs and I went on to work there for ten years and enjoyed every moment of it.

Ed became a self-employed carpenter. My Robin was still at school and coming up to his O levels. Ed was always careful to be nice to Robin's face, but behind his back Ed would tear him to shreds by picking fault with him. Ed was very petty and two-faced. But Robin liked him. Like me, Ed could pull the wool over his eyes. But I learnt the hard way and had a noose around my neck now. It was too late, but in the end I saw through Ed. He was not a nice character. He was a cheat, a liar, and a womaniser. I could fool most people, but not Viv and Betty. They knew I was unhappy, and they could see Ed was not a nice person without me having to tell them.

I thought I had to make the best of a bad thing and got on with it. Next, he conned me into buying our council house. I would get about half knocked off, as I was a long-term sitting tenant, and he would he pay the mortgage, on some kind of endowment. I didn't quite understand it at the time. Plus, he would put something towards the food, and I would have to pay all the utility bills, council tax, phone bills, T.V. and Robin's and my food and clothes. That was alright until the poll tax came in. I was working more hours now to pay my share. He was having forty pound a week for his drink. This was why he had asked me all those questions in the beginning about my house. There were no flies on him.

Then came the biggest con of all. He said that he was working down in Cornwall, and he needed more petrol for his car. He asked me if I would get a second credit card in my name, so that he could get more petrol if he needed it. Like a fool, I did, as he couldn't get credit himself. Then the bills started to come in on my credit card. It was a little more each month, until it reached about three hundred pounds a month. Now, I didn't earn three hundred a month, and I was still expected to pay the other bills. I went to him, 'You are going to have to help me out. You are running up more than I am earning.' 'No,' Ed said. 'The card's in your name. You pay it!'

I thought, 'So that's your game? You've taken me for a patsy again.' Both Viv and Betty could see through me by now and knew I was worried about something. They asked what was wrong and suggested we talk about it after work. I told them what was happening. 'What! You don't earn that much!' 'That is what I am worried about,' I said. 'You can drive now!' They were right. I could by this time. Viv said, 'I can put you in touch with a chap who will help you.' So, I had a talk with this chap. Since I could drive, he showed me how to read the dials. 'Do you have the car on your own anytime?' 'Yes,' I said, 'every Monday evening, but only up and back from the club each week. I take Ed and his friend, because of the drink driving law.' 'That is the time to take the reading,' he said. 'Bring all your receipts and credit bills for the last few months. I will see you in a fortnight, as you need two readings.'

The next time I saw this chap I had everything he wanted. He went through it with me. 'Well, I am sorry to tell you that you are being robbed by your husband and the petrol attendant, as he only gets his petrol at the same station each time. They are both in on the scam. You should take this to the police as I would say he is using about sixty pounds of petrol a month, and he is saying he is using over two hundred pounds a month instead.' 'But I can't do that! I just want to stop him. How can I?' The chap said, 'Get his card and cut it up. What kind of husband have you got, to do this to you?' I said, 'A chauvinistic pig.' So, that evening, I said, 'Ed, I think I need to look at the date on your card. I think it is getting near the time to renew it.' I already had the scissors in my hand. Ed gave me the credit card. I cut up the card in front of him. 'Why did you do that?' he said. 'Because I know you and the petrol attendant have been scamming me. I can take it to the police and get you both in trouble, so watch it!' I had the upper hand. I was silly enough not to divorce him at this time. I knew I couldn't pay off the debt Ed had run up and keep a roof over my head. So, my hands were tied again.

39

This would have been 1988. Robin was at university now. I, in the meantime, worked hard to pay off the debt. It was going down in leaps and bounds and I had nearly got there. Next, Ed tried to get money for his daughter. She was having a baby and going to live with the father of the baby. I asked what that had to do with me? He replied saying he had helped me to bring up Robin! 'When?' I said. 'You never gave me a penny towards his keep, so don't try that on!' Ed was crazy about his daughter. When they were together, they were like lovers with their arms all over each other. He was quite pleased when someone asked one day, 'Is this your girlfriend?' They did not behave like father and daughter. One day she nearly pushed me off the stool so she could sit beside Ed. Then Ed had the cheek to say I was jealous of his daughter. 'You are nothing but an old bag,' he said to me. I said, 'Your daughter is nothing but a rude spoilt brat.' Over the years, his brother and wife and three children would come down every year for their holidays. His brother thanked me for keeping Ed out of the gutter. Although even he was awful at times. I thought if I had known it, I wouldn't have married Ed.

I had to keep his brother's family. Ed never gave me money to help, so every opportunity I had, I would work. Next evening, Roddy asked me to help with the evening-do upstairs, so I said yes. I asked Ed's brother and sister-in-law, 'What meat shall I leave out tomorrow?' He swore at me, 'How do you expect us to know what we will fancy tomorrow?' 'Fair enough,' I said. 'You will have to fend for yourselves. If I don't work, I can't put meals on the table as I don't get any help from your brother, Ed. No money, or any kind of help. I am just a servant, and dog's body here.'

I went out early that morning as I still had my two jobs, to cook breakfast at the hotel, then on to the pub. I came home in the afternoon, cleaned up a bit, had a nap, then back to the pub. I laid the tables and sat down with Roddy and Maggie to have a bite to eat and a nice cup of tea before the evening started. It was hard work being on your feet for six hours. The evening went off well, and the people were pleased. There was a nice big tip, but I felt like running out of the house with the greeting I got when I walked in through the front door.

All of them were on me like a ton of bricks. Their immediate complaint was why their evening meal wasn't done. 'Because I've been working all day to feed you! I don't get any help from you, Ed. And this is not a hotel. I asked you what meat you would like left out yesterday as I had to work this evening, and you said you didn't know what you would fancy today. *You* try and feed five extra people who are not working with you, but against you. Why don't you all push off back to London, where you come from. I am being treated as a servant by you all, in my own home.' Ed tried to stop me going up the stairs, but I nearly pushed him over. That was an easy thing to do since he was the worse for wear in drink. 'And Ed, you can sleep on the settee. I don't want you snoring in my ear tonight,' I added.

Six o'clock the next morning, I was off to work again. I nearly asked Dot if she had a spare room, as I didn't fancy going home and facing that lot. I did my shift at the pub, then went back with Betty, to unwind for an hour, then I went home. I had just got in when the five of them trooped in. The children were sent in the back garden to play and Ed's brother and sister-in-law came in. 'We are very sorry about how we behaved towards you yesterday. We were all like cads, and we should have known that it was not Ed doing everything for us. We should have known that it was you who made our holidays so pleasant, not Ed. We hope we will be welcome back next year, and we promise we will be different. We love our holiday with you. We see everything you do and know Ed takes the glory. We should have known better than that. You are putting your feet up this evening, and we are doing the dinner and the dishes. We are both truly sorry.'

Ed came home and started on me again. 'Leave her alone,' his brother said. 'Well, she didn't pack my lunch this morning!' His brother exclaimed, 'She has to pack your lunch up every day?' 'Of course, or I don't go to work!' 'You idle git!' said his brother. 'Don't start again,' I said, 'I know Ed and his daughter want me out but they've got a hard fight on their hands and I am not going. Right from the day we married, Ed and his daughter have been trying to get me out. The times I've been told I am jealous of his daughter.' 'Why?' his brother asked. 'Because she's a model and pretty, and I am an old

134

bag!' 'What! Never!' From that day on we became the best of friends until the day they both died. It was the same with his ex-wife, too. She would often phone me. We had one rule; we never talked about Ed.

In the meantime, they were trying to get my Robin to go to Oxford, because he had six A levels and I can't remember how many O levels. But Robin wanted to go to Swansea, to be near Rosie's in-laws, Jean and Joe. He was happy there from 1985 until 1988. Robin came away with his Bachelor of Science in Electronics with 1st Degree honours. I went to his graduation and stayed the night at Swansea University. I came down to breakfast to find mostly foreign students looking for Robin's Mum! They stared crowding around me to thank you for bringing up such a lovely son. 'We wouldn't have got our degree without his help!' they said. 'You must have been a good mother!' I never had so many hugs and kisses in my whole life as I did in that short time. It was overwhelming. I wished the girls could have had their share because it was not just me. I shed tears of pride for Robin, for the way he had helped these students, just as the girls and I had helped him when he was a little boy. What more can a Mother ask of her children.

Then Robin went on to London and got his Master of Science from 1988 to 1989, and then his Doctor of Science from 1989 to 1992. This was the little boy they wanted to go to a *backward school*, as they called it, but Robin did owe a lot to his two sisters and myself for helping him so much in the beginning. Robin's aim was to beat his brother Paul, as he had looked up to him. He did it with flying colours. Robin worked so hard for that. But sadly, since 1996, he has hardly given me the time of day, thanks to Ed smearing my name. But Robin has always had time for his brother and sisters, which I have got to be thankful for.

40

Let me get back to Ed and finish his story! I became, and still am, good friends with his ex-sister-in-law, on his ex-wife's side. She came to stay with us a lot after she lost her husband. She opened up and has told me lots over the years. Some of it was not very nice. But there was nothing I had not worked out for myself. That his daughter had some kind of hold over him, the sister-in-law just confirmed. Ed himself would tell me things about his ex-wife and daughter when his tongue got loose with drink. I do believe this; he told me about his daughter, because she was a right little minx. Ed was in the bath when his daughter came into the bathroom, showed him her privates, pulling it open with her fingers, 'Look Dad, I am sore here!' She was fifteen! How many girls could do that in front of their father? It is sick. Or is it me being very naïve?

I came home from work feeling ill one day. I got Ed his dinner and put it in the oven to keep it hot. 'Would you please wash up,' I asked, 'I'm going to bed.' 'No, you're not. You wait there until I finish, and *you* can wash up. Men don't wash up. It's not a man's job!' he retorted. 'So, I'm your servant?' I asked. 'Yes, you've got it in a nutshell!' Ed said. 'I am the only one that can be ill in this house!' Where had I heard *that* before!

Ed's friend, Tony, and Mable his wife, who became my friend, suggested we go on holiday together. I thought I had some insurance money I could take out early. I knew I would lose a bit on it, but it would be nice to have a holiday. I had never been abroad before. So off we went with Mable and Tony to Majorca. If it wasn't for Mable and Tony, the holiday would have been a washout for me.

Ed was drunk every night, so I had to deal the money out nightly or he would have spent it all in one go. One evening we went on a coach trip for a supper as part of the holiday deal. When we got to the place, Ed started showing off. He bought the whole coach a drink, with my money. I thought, 'This man's sick!' It turned out he didn't have enough money to pay the bill and I didn't have any money on me. Luckily, Tony bailed him out, but Ed always had to show off. He was the big man with all the money or shall I say other people's money. Another evening we all went to a dance. Mable and Tony had an early night and went back to their accommodation. I stayed on with Ed, but I got very embarrassed, because Ed wouldn't take his eye off this woman. When this woman pulled her dress off her shoulders, nearly showing her boobs, looked at Ed and said, 'Have you seen enough now?' he just gawked at her in a drunken stupor.

The next evening the four of us went to the dance again. Ed spotted the young woman and played up to her all evening. Tony and Mable were ready to go back to their accommodation. I asked, 'Can you come with me, to see if we can get Ed away from that women, Mable?' Over we went. I said to Ed, 'It's time to go, we've got an early start tomorrow.' Ed said, 'F--- off, you old bag.' I just turned my back on him and went back to the room and locked our door. He was not long behind us. I couldn't leave him outside shouting, so I had to let him in. 'You can sleep on the floor. You disgust me!' 'Why did you spoil my chance with that women?' he asked. 'You can have any women you like; it won't worry me as long as you push off altogether.'

Next day, we set off for our boat trip. Ed was talking to a German couple. His wife was a tall gorgeous blond. Ed couldn't take his eyes off her. The husband came over to me. He was short, fat and ugly. 'Your husband is getting on well with my wife!' he said. 'We could change partners for the day!' Then the penny dropped. 'Could we? I don't think so.' I walked away in disgust. The German came up to me again. 'I've got two rooms at the town we are visiting.' 'I don't care, I don't want you.' I said. 'Your husband won't like it!' said the German. I said, 'Pity!' and walked away again. The boat was about to dock.

We were to have a barbecue on the beach. I left them on their own and walked to the beach. Ed followed me. 'What do you think you're playing at?' he said. 'I was getting on well with that blond. My type of girl!' 'What was stopping you?' I said. I could see Ed was not a happy bunny when he answered me. 'Her husband went off with another couple. You are a proper spoil sport!' I was getting a bit uptight by now. 'How dare you put me on the spot like that. I don't care if he was drop down gorgeous, I am no slut, even if you are. The way you are behaving on this holiday disgusts me. You have spoilt this holiday for me.'

When we got back from our holiday, I gave him his marching orders. This is when what Ed and his daughter were up to all came out. Ed said, 'You can't get rid of me. It's my home.' He had never put a piece of furniture or anything else into the house. It was Robin's and mine, right down to last cup. (My advice to anyone thinking they would like to get remarried is; it doesn't matter how little they have, take out a prenuptial so that you don't lose everything. Keep a roof over your heads.) I asked him to leave again. 'No! It is you that are leaving.' I said, 'I am not. This is my home.

I said to Ed, 'I can have you up for non-consummation of our marriage.' Ed said, 'How can you prove it? You have been a married woman. You had children!' Ed had me over a barrel, I think, but then again, maybe not. There might have been a way of telling, as I hadn't had sex since 1972, when Roger became ill, and we were in 1992 now. But Ed didn't know anything of my sex life. We never talked about it. As I said, all those questions he asked me before we married, about the house, proves Ed was just after my home. I was hoping he would go off with one of his many girlfriends. But, no luck. I was stuck with him.

My Rosie, her husband and little Zoe were coming down for a few days. 'Not those, cadgers?' Ed said. 'What do mean by that?' I asked. Ed said, 'They are always on the take!' 'Oh, come off it,' I said, 'They have only ever had birthday and Christmas presents. It's your daughter that keeps us poor, always on the want. It is like she's got some kind of hold over you.' 'There you are; jealous of her again!' Ed said. 'Don't talk rot. She's got nothing I am jealous about. Tell me why I have got to be jealous of her? Don't say my age. She's already got pimples all over her face now when she takes all that make up off. Wait until she reaches my age! It is going to look like orange peel.' At last I shot him down. It was the only way I could fight against Ed.

All the time Rosie was there he was sweetness himself, and all over Zoe. He couldn't say enough nice things about them to their face. But he stabbed them in the back when they were out of earshot. Ed's daughter was on the phone interfering again. 'My Dad should be playing golf.' 'What on?' I said to Ed, 'Shirt buttons?' Next, she was trying to tell me how I should run my home, and what I should be doing, and how it should be done. What was she trying to do? Squeeze more money out of us? Pompous little git. Who does she think she is speaking to?' By this time, I was working extra hours. Ed never did any overtime; he was a very lazy man. He wouldn't even do anything to help. I had to mow the grass, cut the hedges, tidy the garden, do all the housework and cooking. He would just leave his dirty clothes on the floor where he took them off.

One day I left it there. I just washed the household things and my clothes, ironed them and put them away. I did this for a few days, then came Friday. 'Where's my clean shirt?' 'I don't know. I did all the washing in the wash basket. I only do washing that's in the basket! I am fed up of picking up after you. You're nothing but a lazy git. Oh, and by the way, you can pack your own lunch box from now on.' 'Well, I won't go to work then,' said Ed. I said, 'Please yourself. If you don't pay the mortgage, you will lose the house. You will have to pay all your own taxes. I pay mine as I go. They get taken out of my wages every week. If we lose the house, I will just get myself a flat. You have pushed me around long enough. And you can tell this to your daughter.'

All Ed could think about was the drink and his daughter; he never thought of his son. He was a lovely young man; I liked him. He was a son to be proud of, but sadly we didn't see a lot of him, only the daughter. She was down a lot, with her airs and graces. She always expected me to wait on her hand and foot. But the tide had turned.

I stayed out of her way, by going out to meals with some of my friends. After work I went to the pictures, anything but go home. When I got home, Ed said, 'There is no food in the cupboard.' 'I am not running after her; I am just proving to her I can't run a home. It's *your* place. She's your daughter. It was she who said I can't run a home. When she's gone, I will be here to cook and clean again. How much longer is she staying?' 'She's going home tomorrow.' 'Good! Tomorrow we are going to Tesco. We will do the shopping once a week. No more am I going into town and carting the shopping on the bus and up that steep hill, while you are whizzing up the hill past me with a carload of girls about thirteen and fourteen years old. Or any young lady that you fancy. That is coming to a stop.'

41

Roddy and Maggie had moved on. We were sad to see them go. A new tenant had taken over the pub, and shortly after, Viv and I were made redundant, because of our age. They were going to take on a younger staff after the pub was done up. With the help of a solicitor who always came in at lunch times, Viv and I were told to take them to court for ageism. He put us onto the right people to fight the case for us.

I got seven thousand, plus two thousand and a little work pension. I was also working as an Avon lady and was doing ironing for a customer. This lady said, 'I hear you lost your job?' 'I am looking for something else,' I replied. 'Well, I am a matron in a nursing home, and I could do with more good staff. Would you like a job with me?' 'Do you think I can do it?' I asked. 'Why not give it a try? she said, 'and see if you like it,' which I did. This is when I should have left Ed. But no. I wanted my home back. Shortly after, Ed said there was no work around.

This did happen from time to time. I got Ed to build a built-in bedroom, and a new kitchen, all from M.F.I. You could buy the units for a few hundred. Things were much cheaper then. We did all the work ourselves, including a new bath with shower. We had to have a plumber to fit the central heating and do the plumbing. I know that sounds a lot, but even the plumber did it cheaply, because he was just starting out on own and he needed a show house. By doing the other work ourselves, with Tony doing the electrics, all our labour was free. It was only the cost of the material we had to pay for which I think it came to just over two thousand.

I loved working up at the nursing home. It was nice caring for people, but sad when they passed away. There were many times I went home with a tear in my eye. I soon took on night work. It was a long shift, but I soon got used to it. I was now in my late fifties and it was 1993. In less than a year I would get my pension and a bus pass. With Ed still out of work, I had to pay the mortgage, Ed's stamp, his private pension, and his pocket money, and extra petrol money, as he needed it to go after the jobs. Money was flying out now. With very little left, a friend told me, 'I saw Ed today! He was in the bar most of the day, chatting the bar maid up. I was working across the road all day.' 'Oh, is that his little game!' I exclaimed.

The first thing I did was to move five hundred to another account. That was for a rainy day. I would have put more in if I had known what he was up to sooner. Then I cut his beer money by half. That hurt. I couldn't do it all to once. I said, 'Next week, I will have to cut your spending money again as the tax is due on your car next. I will pay six months on that. I've got this month's mortgage, your private pension, and enough for another month. The rest is up to you.' The next day he got a job. That got him moving. Ed had been sponging off me for months. The greater part of my money had gone. He was not going to work until all my money was gone. What kind of fool was I, that I couldn't see through him? All this time he had been out womanising and spending my money. All *I* was trying to do, was to keep my home.

I was happy at my work and looked forward to going in every evening. When I got home one morning, the phone rang, and who was on the phone? His daughter! This was a one off. She said, 'You shouldn't be working nights!' I asked why. 'My dad needs a wife.' I knew what she was getting at, so I said, 'What cock and bull story has your dad been telling you now? He has made it obvious to me that he prefers you rather than me. I am an old bag to him. He likes his women a lot younger. Your father has never consummated our marriage. We sleep in separate rooms now since he took to wetting the bed from too much drink. He has never kissed me on the lips. Now and again he will kiss me on the cheek, to show others what a loving husband he is. What a laugh! Ed is just a cold fish. All I get is you, you and more of you. Over and over, again and again in my ear. Telling me that I am jealous of you. I've got nothing to be jealous of. You come into my home and treat me like I am dirt. I wouldn't like to have a character like yours. It was not the kind of thing I was brought up to do.' His daughter said lamely, 'Well, I thought you weren't nice to dad.' I said, 'I know you are both trying to hound me out of my home.' And I slammed the phone down.

In 1993, Rosie and David gave me another granddaughter; my little Vicky. They came to see me. She was lovely and it was great to see them all again. Zoe was growing away but I made a fuss of her. But they were only down for a few days. I missed them when they went back. It was about the end of 1994. I got my government pension, but I didn't let on to Ed I had it. I started to keep things to myself, but he was very greedy and had extravagant taste. I was putting more and more money into the house. With everything going up, including all the utility bills and food, there was hardly enough to feed me. I lived on one egg and a few chips for my dinner most days. But that still didn't stop the bills going up. Once or twice a year, I would save up to go to the theatre with Mable, but in the end, I had to apologise to her. 'I can't afford it, Mable.' She offered to treat me. 'No thanks, Mable.' I replied sadly. 'It's Ed. If I go out of an evening, he wants twenty pounds so he can go out too. He doesn't like staying at home on his own. That's nearly seven hours more work for me, to get that amount of money, and I am not doing it. I am already doing sixty to seventy hours a week. What does he want; blood out of a stone?'

That wasn't the only way Ed tried to get more money out of me. Ed, Tony, Mable, and I went up the club once a month, as there was a dance. I would have to drive them home, so that they could drink. This was all free for him since I paid his yearly subs. Ed would buy me a ginger ale, which cost about twenty pence. Ed and Tony would go to another room to play pool. Mable and I didn't care. We enjoyed the dancing and music. When we got home that evening, he said, 'From now on, I will need an extra twenty pounds when you come out with me.' I said, 'What for? One ginger ale? On your bike! I would sooner stay home,' I said, as he turned to walk away from me. Is your daughter putting the squeeze on you again?' I think I was right, she had some kind of hold over him. I shouted after him, 'If it is going to be like that, from now on you and Tony can walk up and back to the club, as I won't drive you up and back anymore. And by the way, you can pay your own subs from now on too, and I will stay home.' I told Mable what happened. 'So, I will not be up anymore, Mable.' 'What a pity!' she said. 'Would *you* pay it?' I asked her. 'No!' was her immediate reply, 'It's blackmail.' When she then added, 'He is such a lovely man,' it sounded as if she thought it was my fault. I wondered

143

where she was coming from. Even when we were on holiday together and he swore at me, in front of her, she said it was only the drink! That's what Ed was like. He could charm the birds off the trees.

42

1995 was when my health took a downward slide. I went to the doctors. She said I needed a better diet, and fewer working hours. 'I have such a poor diet and work so many hours, because my husband demands more and more. I must keep us out of debt,' I explained. 'What you are telling me is nothing short of mental cruelty. I don't normally say this, but you would be better if you divorced him.' I said, 'He won't leave. *I* would have to go, and my husband will win in the end.' The doctor said, 'It is that, or your health.' I went to see the solicitor and told him my plight. He said, 'It would be hard to prove mental cruelty. All it boils down to is your word against his. The best grounds are irretrievable break down. If you give up your work, I can get this on the green card. Most likely, you would get half.' I thought, half of what? 'I don't want to give up my work. I love it, and I think I would be more likely to get a flat if I am working. I don't want to be made homeless.' The solicitor said, 'You can do it on your own. I will help you fill the form in at a price.' This was fair, as he helped me a lot. He set the petition out. When I faced Ed with the petition, he said, 'I am not signing that. You are going to carry on working to keep me!'

'I am not,' I said, 'if you don't sign this petition, I will give up work, and go on the green card. The solicitor and doctor will both fight for my divorce. This would mean we will both lose. The house will be sold, plus the contents, the car that I've been paying for will have to go and everything else. By the time the solicitor has his fee, there is not going to be a lot left over for us. But, please yourself.' I must say there was a little bit of bluff on my side, as I didn't know if the doctor could help. Ed said, 'I must phone my daughter first.' She was in on this all along. I knew it.

Ed said, 'I will sign the petition, but only if my daughter agrees. Then I will sign and keep the house.' I said, 'That's not fair. This was my home, before you came along.' But I knew I couldn't keep up the mortgage as Ed had taken out another endowment to clear a huge tax bill he had run up before he came down from London. He had taken thousands out. I think it was fifteen thousand to cover it in all. I don't think his daughter knew this. All she thought was that her dad wasn't going to make old bones, and if he stayed married to me, she would have to wait until I died. And even then, she would only get a part share and not half. She was just greedy. She wanted a bigger cut.

I got home just after eight in the morning and went to bed. I was not cooking for Ed now. When I got up, I made myself something to eat and watched a bit of telly. Ed came in and said he would sign the petition. I thought, here it comes! He has been talking to madam again. 'I want the house and all the contents and the car,' he said. I looked up to him, 'You just want jam on it!' This is an old saying that we had when people wanted too much. I didn't know what else to say. I was flabbergasted. Ed wanted everything. He might as well throw me out on the street there and then. He was trying to rob me of everything.

I walked out of the room and went to my bedroom. I just cried and cried. How was I going to fight this? What kind of people were they? At that moment all I could do was cry. I sobbed my heart out. To think I stuck this unhappiness out for twelve years, and he still won. No wonder I was upset. In the evening, I had such a headache from crying so much that I went downstairs. I made a cup of tea. I thought I would take two paracetamol when the tea cooled down. I took it all up stairs with me, to see if I could sleep.

But when I put the two tablets on my hand, I could see they were not paracetamol. At that time, Boots always sold the paracetamol and aspirin in the same size brown bottles. I had picked up the aspirin by mistake. I was so frustrated, I threw them all over the floor, as I am allergic to aspirin. They rolled everywhere and I was left with nothing for my headache. I just drank my tea and laid on my bed. I couldn't sleep right away as I was tossing this way and that over the idea, of whether to do what the solicitor said; to give up my job and go on the green card, and let him fight it for me. At least I would come out with the same as Ed. I had a smile on my face as I went to sleep.

I didn't hear Ed come with a cup of tea for me; the first ever in twelve years. Why now? Ed thought I had committed suicide, with so many aspirins on the floor. Is this what they were hoping for? Instead of calling for an ambulance, which didn't make sense, he called my Lydia. I was just waking from a good sleep when Lydia came into my bedroom. I said, 'What are you doing here?' 'Ed phoned me, to say you have committed suicide.' That is what they were hoping, maybe. This old bird is made of stouter stuff than that. I told Lydia everything. 'They are not doing that to you, Mum!' said Lydia. 'You get dressed and I will make a cuppa.'

I went downstairs. There was Ed, sitting at the table, all bleary eyed from too much drink the night before. Lydia had already told me to leave it to her, so I just sat there sipping my tea. 'So, you and your daughter want to take everything away from my Mum? Well, that is not going to happen. You are not going to rob her of everything, while I am alive! First, Mum wants one of the two endowments; she would like the smaller one. We want you to sign it over right away. Next, Mum is going to take any of the contents she might need, for her new flat. Everything in this house Mum bought before you came. Next is all the presents we have given her over the years. You are not having them.' Ed said, 'I need to phone my daughter.' 'This has got nothing to do with your daughter. She has done enough damage,' Lydia said. 'And I haven't finished yet. If you don't agree to Mum's terms, she is going to take it to court, and I will be there as a witness, and you might end up with nothing, Ed. It is up to you. Now, go and phone your daughter. He was on the phone for a while. 'I will agree with all the terms, and I will sign the petition. Lydia wrote down everything we agreed on, and he signed. 'If you go back on your word, we will just take it to court.' Good for Lydia!

'I will be there on the day you move, Mum,' said Lydia, 'to see you get everything that is yours.' 'Thank you, Lydia.' I found a little one bedroom flat back in the Efford Estate, just up the road from where I used to live. That was fine, as it was all I could afford, and it would all be paid off in a few years' time. There was a small payment each month, on the endowment. I had to borrow four thousand for a mortgage. As you can see there were very small repayments on it all.

The divorce came through in January 1996, but before I left the house, Ed asked if he could keep the bedroom furniture if he built me a built-in bedroom, and did other works I might need in the flat. We agreed. I told him he could keep all the furniture. It wouldn't fit in my small flat anyway. I still had that five hundred, plus a little I managed to salt away, when I found out that Ed and his daughter had in mind to take everything. They had both had enough out of me. I have written about my life with Ed. His words were very abusive, sometimes worse than a slap across a face. *That* would only hurt for a short while, but the words cut deep.

I was never young enough for Ed, even though he was only fourteen months younger than me. But Ed liked women who were about twenty or even younger. We were both in our late forties at that time. So why did he marry me? Was it for the house? Or did he see the mug in me? Or both? I only stayed there to try and keep my and Robin's home. This is what the judge awarded in the divorce settlement from Roger. Robin still had a room here, though he was not home much at this time. Ed was still very careful not to show his abusive side towards me to anyone, including my family. He came over as being Mr Nice Man.

Ed came around most Saturdays to do the work he had promised. I was to give him dinner. It took him six months to put my bedroom together, a breakfast bar in the kitchen, and some shelves in the under-stair's cupboard. I got friendly with the lady upstairs. We still are to this day! 'I don't hear much work going on while you're shopping, so I thought I would sweep our pathway,' she said. 'I peeped in your window and he was sat in your armchair, watching sport on your T.V. and drinking beer. I hope you don't mind. Please, don't think I am a nosey parker.' 'Oh no! Thanks a lot. From then on, I changed my shopping day to Friday, with Mable. After that the work moved along.

I had some very good news. My grandson was born. I was looking forward to seeing him soon, but it was sooner than expected, as Rosie was needed back at work. I was able to get a week off to look after Geo and Vicky. She loved me there, only because I told her the names of the birds and flowers. All too soon I had to come back to work.

I was making curtains and things for the home, also doing the garden. Maude asked me to do her bit of garden out the front. She called herself my labourer. She cleaned up behind me and did the watering every evening. The gardens soon looked a picture. Out the back in my plot, I grew my veggies and fruit. I shared everything with Maude upstairs and if I was working in the garden she would come with her bacon sandwiches and a cup of tea, saying I never stopped working!

Eventually, I had had enough of Ed hanging around, so I told him straight, 'What I have given you in food, could pay for someone to do the jobs twice over!' Ed said, 'I should finish next week.' 'About time!' I said. Sure enough, he did. Ed asked me out the following Sunday afternoon, and most Sunday afternoons after, but there was a catch! I had to pay for lunch, and he paid for the petrol. It gave me chance to go bird watching, and to keep my driving up. Actually, it was quite pleasant. We went out around Tor Cross, Thursden Beach, and all the little villages around there. We saw the grebes mating on Slapton Lye, I had never seen that before. It was a lovely place for bird watching, but Ed was becoming a nuisance. He was always on the cadge for food, with cheese, ham and bread most days for his lunches. So, I stopped going out with him. I wasn't going to keep him. As a tradesman, he could earn three times more than me for a forty-hour week. I was working seventy-seven hours for a third of his wages, and he was coming to me for food!

43

It was coming up to November. I was going up to Rosie's for my birthday. I would also take their Christmas presents at the same time, as I was working over the Christmas so that mums with children could have time off from work. I set off that day with two heavy cases. I got to North Road Station. It was a bit of a struggle getting up the steps because the cases were so heavy. I looked at the long underpass to platform seven and wondered if I could make it. Then a voice came from behind, 'Can I help you, Mam?' I turned and said, 'Yes, please.' thinking it was a porter. But he was just a gentleman. It turned out he really was a gentleman! I went to hand him one case and he took both. 'What platform?' 'Seven, please.' When we got to platform seven, this gentleman said, 'What time is your train?' 'Just over an hour,' I said, 'I allowed extra time because my cases were so heavy.' He asked me if I would like a cup of tea and I said yes. We got talking. He had lost his wife in August. I was sorry to hear that. He seemed just an elderly, lonely gent. We chatted some more. 'I see you are not wearing a wedding ring,' he said. 'I have been divorced since January this year,' I replied. 'Where are you going to now?' he asked. 'Up to see my daughter, son-in-law and three grandchildren.' This gent said he had not been blessed with children. 'I am so sorry to hear that,' I said. 'I find them such a blessing, and expensive, this time of the year! That is why my cases are so heavy. I have got their Christmas presents in them as I won't be seeing them over Christmas since I am working.'

'Do you like walking?' he asked. 'I love it. I have always wanted to walk the moors. We used to drive around there, but never walk.' 'That's funny!' he said, 'that is where I would love to take you!' 'But I am still working!' I replied quickly. 'You could come on your days off!' 'That would be lovely,' I said. 'By the way, what's your name?' he asked. 'Faith, and yours?' 'Philip. So, can I phone you when you get home?' 'Yes, please. But make it before six o'clock in the evenings, as I am a night worker.' I gave him my phone number and I told him the date I would be back. Then the train pulled in, and I was off to Basingstoke. He waved me goodbye. I had a lovely week with Rosie. I was spoilt. We went to Swanage for a day which was such a pretty place. But the week soon went by, and it was back to work again.

I had been home for a day when the phone rang. It was Philip, asking if we could meet the next day. He said it was too cold to go walking on the moors, and suggested we meet in town for a cup of tea and asked if I knew of a place we could go to. I replied, 'If I go out with my friend Mable, we always go down to the basement of the Co-op. There is a lovely little café, tucked in the corner.' We agreed to meet at two, and we said our goodbyes. I was thinking about Philip that evening. He struck me as a very lonely gent, about seventy, his wife gone, no children, and in need of company, like a lot of the elderly people where I worked; just someone to talk to and tell their little story to. I think I was the right person he needed at this time. I think I was sent to help him. All he needed was a bit of my time. There I go! One of my feelings again!

I met Philip the next day. He had one red rose for me. I thought, 'How sweet!' He seemed so pleased to see me and wouldn't let me pay for the tea. He was the perfect gentleman. We talked. I told him about my time in Basingstoke, and how I had a wonderful time with my family. I said I missed them, and that it was a pity we lived so far apart as they were lovely and fun to be with. Philip told me about himself. He had worked in the dockyard all his life, even in the war. He was exempt, having had T.B. in his late teens. He said he would have loved to have gone into the air force. Philip, as I said before was the perfect gentleman, opening doors for me and always walking on the outside of the pavement when he was with me. I had never been treated like this in my life. He was a very lovely man.

We met a few times before Christmas. 'As you know, I am working extra hours over the Christmas and I can't let these people down, since they have children,' I said to Philip. He replied, 'I have also got long standing arrangements at Christmas and New Year. I am going out to my brother's for Christmas, and to friends for the New Year.' 'That will be nice for you!' I said. 'I am also going out on New Year's Eve. Like yours, they are long standing arrangements. My friend, Mable, bought the tickets. I thought just three of us were going but she told me my ex is coming too.' Philip face dropped. 'I wouldn't go back with him for all the tea in China. I was going to invite you around on the second day in 1997 for dinner about three o'clock! Don't forget I must be at work by nine!' His face lit up, 'We can arrange to speak on the phone, and I must give you my address.'

I enjoyed Mable's company. The men went off to play pool and Mable and I spent a lovely evening, enjoying the music, and dancing, and singing. About eleven o'clock, the men joined us. Tony came back and took Mable out on the dance floor. It was obvious this was prearranged. I was left with Ed. I was one side of the table and he was the other side, drinking beer. I was just watching the dancers and singing along to the music. Tony brought Mable back to the table. The next dance is going to be the twist and, as Mable hated the twist, Tony said, 'Come on, Faith! This is our dance!' and he pulled me onto the dance floor. We came back panting but laughing. It was fun. Tony and Mable went on the dance floor again. The tune was 'Always On My Mind'. When it came to the part of the song, '*I treated you second best*', Ed said, 'That is what I did to you,' 'Yes, but that is an understatement. Your daughter was first, last, and in-between. You both wanted me out and took everything from me. You were both con artists.'

He was really crying in his beer. 'But my daughter hardly phones me now, and the house is not a home anymore.' 'I expect she got you to change your will right away, in favour of her and your son!' 'Yes,' said Ed. 'I thought so!' I said, 'that's all she wanted.' Ed said, 'I didn't think I would miss you so much, or your cooking, Faith.' I said, 'You didn't know which side your bread was buttered, did you?' I didn't give him chance to answer. 'I hope you are not thinking about asking me back, as that is like rubbing salt into the wound. Forget it, as I have just met a man in a million. He knows how to treat a woman. He is much kinder and nicer than you ever have been to me. In fact, he is a perfect gentleman.' I was really rubbing it in. Why not, after what he put me through? 'Right from the start, on our wedding day, you left me for three hours with our guests, just to be with you daughter. How did you think I felt that day? You didn't give a damn. As for being jealous of your daughter, no way. Her beauty is skin deep.' Now me being catty, I added, 'By the way, have you seen her without her makeup? As you said, she has got you to change your will, all she has got to do now is to wait for you to drink yourself to death.' I was really being nasty. It was right out of character for me.

I carried on. 'She almost said this one day to me, that I would outlive you.' '*He is going to drink himself to death,*' she said. That is why she needed me out of the picture. She doesn't want you, just the money.' (He died in 2000. She only had to wait just over three years.) I said goodbye. 'I don't want to see you anymore.' I could see I had hurt him, but not as much as he had hurt me in those twelve years. He would never change. He never loved me. He never would, even if I went back to him. A leopard never changes his spots. He cheated and robbed me blind. Not just money, but my health. And all for his daughter. What kind of hold did she have on him? I know it is God's way to forgive. But how many times have you got to turn the other cheek? In the end, I forgave them both. These three men ruined my life. I should have just forgiven them and walked away. I was a soft fool, to have taken them back time and time again.

After that, Ed started to blacken my name with lies. It didn't worry me one bit. The old saying is: 'sticks and stones can break my bones, but names will never hurt me.' But when he tried to blacken Philip's name, that was another matter. Ed was spreading it around that I was seeing Philip thirteen months before I put in for a divorce.

Ed even told Pauline, my next-door neighbour, who also worked up the nursing home. Pauline said, 'When did she have time to go out with other men? The girls and I pulled her leg about it, telling her she should bring her bed up here. I know she has been working about seventy hours a week. I know for a fact she would come home, tidy the garden, cut the grass and hedges, then I could hear the cleaner going With these walls being paper thin I even know when she is cooking the evening meal! You are nothing but a lazy, good-for-nothing; a drunkard and liar, and you are trying to take that good woman's name away. I will tell everyone around here that you are a liar. You were not just satisfied in taking her home away, but also her good name.'

I also had a go at Ed over the phone. 'I don't worry for myself about what you are spreading around, but it's the allegations you are making about this kind gent I know. It's not fair. At the time of your allegations, this man was nursing a sick wife who had a stroke and died in August 1996. I met him at the station when he was kind enough to carry my two heavy cases for me, when I went up to see Rosie in November. You should be careful because this man could have you up for libel. Right now, he is still grieving for his dead wife, and I am grieving over the loss of my home. Right now, we are consoling each other. There is nothing more than that between us.'

But Ed had not finished with me yet. The next thing he tried was to turn my children against me. Lydia simply showed Ed the door. Rosie said to him, 'I don't care what my Mum is supposed to have done; she's my Mum and I couldn't wish for a better one.' On the other hand, Ed turned Robin against me. How? I don't know. Robin couldn't have had a more devoted mother. I did everything possible to help him as baby. I walked the floor with him night after night wishing I could take the pain away from him. I had all the love and patience a mother can sum up even when she is ready to drop herself; sometimes neglecting the three older children. Fortunately, they understood.

When Robin was older and wanted to learn to read and write, he had three of us dancing around him, attending to him with his good readers; more Rosie than anyone. I was the one that got him into mainstream school. I was the one who showed him how to do his figures and letters, and helped with his maths, and nursed him when he was ill. When he wanted me to take him away from his father, I did. I went to Teignmouth, found a job and a flat. Then he turned around to me and said he wanted to go back to Plymouth, to his own school, and I did that too. The only thing Ed could have used to turn Robin against me was religion, as Robin was a born-again Christian. I had already admitted I had committed adultery earlier in my story, but I had never told Ed. (good job I didn't, as I would never have heard the last of it.) All he knew was that I was married to Roger and divorced him, but this is the kind of thing Ed would have used, to turn Robin off me. I think this is what he did, as Robin made a remark once that he did not like Philip despite not even having met him. God is my judge, and no one else, and as Jesus said, 'Let them that have not sinned, cast the first stone.' It is up to God to judge me and punish me.

I have been punished by Robin for over twenty years. I never heard him call me 'Mum' since, and how it hurts. I still cry over it. I remember when Rosie and Robin would fight over who would sit bedside me. In the end, I would sit in the middle of the settee, so that they could sit either side of me. Sometimes, I wish we could turn back the hands of time to when my Robin loved me. I wish that Robin was more like Rosie and Lydia and had not believed Ed's lies. I forgive him, and it doesn't matter if he hurts me; I will still love him. But Robin, of all people, should have known how messy divorces can be. He had heard the way his father lied about me saying that I was a bad mother, because he wanted custody of Robin. I really had to fight hard for Robin. As I am writing this in 2019, Robin has at last called me Mum. Thank you, God.

44

Philip came for his late Christmas dinner. He enjoyed it. 'You're a good cook, Faith!' I said thank you and went to do the dishes. Philip followed me to the kitchen and picked up the tea towel and started wiping the dishes. 'There is no need for you to help me,' I said. 'The quicker the dishes get done, the quicker we sit down together to talk!' he said. As I made a cup of tea, he said, 'You need a few jobs done here! I hope that's not out of line.' 'I know they need doing, but I need to wait until I've got a bit more money together. A little at a time, until I get it just as I want it.' But Philip said, 'We will see about that! The next rainy day, I shall be down here with my tools.'

I played some of my CDs. 'I like your taste in music, Faith.' 'I have got a lot more,' I said, 'but they are 78's and LPs and I have nothing to play them on.' 'You will have to bring them out to my place to play them,' was his answer. Philip bought me a weather-proof coat for Christmas. 'I wanted to buy some boots for you, as you will need them for walking the moors, but I didn't know your size.' 'You're spoiling me!' I exclaimed. Philip said, 'I am not! I will get the pleasure of your company. You need to be dressed properly, as the weather can change so quickly on the moors.' I asked if we were going on my next day off. 'Yes, if the weather is right.' 'Oh, look at the time! It's flown, it's time for work and I must get ready,' I said. 'I will drop you off on my way home,' Philip replied. I said thank you and he quickly said, 'No, I should be for thanking you for that lovely meal.' Philip took me to work and we said our goodbyes with a hug.

As I went around doing my work, I heard, 'Oh, you're in tonight, Faith. Will you put my stockings on in the morning, please?' It was Reg. He had to wear compression stockings right up to his thighs. I had the knack to get the rucks out because if you didn't, it made sores on your legs. I had learned this from all that wore these compression stockings, dear folk. It wasn't my job, it was a job for the day staff, but if it brought them comfort, that is what we were there for.

There was a dear old lady who had dementia. She was awake most of the night, so I would go in with a cuppa, and just sit, holding her hand, and feeding her with her cup of tea, with her smacking her lips. One day, I was on duty, and her husband came in, and said, 'This must be hard for you.' He said she was a lovely lady who had entertained the troops in the war as a singer. She had a lovely voice. 'Do you want a cup of tea and biscuit?' 'Yes, please.' 'I will bring one in for Elsie, but shall I give it her or you?' 'You, please,' he said. I gave Elsie her tea. 'Was that nice, Elsie?' I said, and she smacked her lips. Her husband was moved, 'I have not seen her do that for a while.' 'Do you speak to her? I asked. 'No!' he said. 'Why not try whispering sweet nothings when I am gone and hold her hand,' I suggested.

Next, he was coming out of matron's room. 'Mr. so-and-so has told me you spend time with Elsie?' she said. 'Yes, every night I go in and talk to her, and give her a cup of tea, and hold her hand, and Elsie makes small facial responses.' I told her husband to say goodbye, as he would at home, not forgetting to catch hold of her hand. He said goodbye and all three of us actually saw it, just that little sign. After that I sang Elsie the war songs, holding her hand every night. I am sure I brought a little comfort in her last hours. The girls thought I was potty.

At six o'clock every evening, Philip phoned. I looked forward to these calls. He had been to see his friends and I had been out with Mable. Philip and I were going to meet the next day. 'I have got your boots and some thick socks, and the weather is looking good for tomorrow!' 'That's good,' I said, 'I am really looking forward to it.' 'Me too,' said Philip, 'See you at ten o'clock tomorrow, bye!' It was Thursday at last and Philip was here on time. He had packed us a lunch and wanted me to try on the boots. I put the socks on, then the boots. They were a lovely fit. 'I bought the boots a half size bigger, because of the thick socks, I hope that's alright.' It was!

I felt spoilt in my new coat and boots. Philip drove us to the edge of the moors to somewhere called Cadover Bridge. 'This is an easy walk for your first walk in new boots,' Philip said. 'We don't want to overdo it. Tell me when you have had enough, and we will sit down.' What with the boots being very comfortable and being well wrapped up and warm in this new weather-proof coat, I had no trouble at all. We found a nice sheltered spot for lunch with the sun shining on us, the birds singing and the ripple of the water as we sat there eating our banquet! I had never seen so much food. I wondered how he got all that in his backpack, plus a flask of hot tea. We sat there and talked.

Then Philip asked me why I needed to work so many hours. 'Well, it's a long story. It hurts me to talk about it, and I don't want to spoil our lovely day. All I will tell you now is that I had to start all over again at the age of sixty. I have got a few debts which I need to clear. When I clear them, I can cut back on the hours. Please leave it at that.' Philip said, 'Can I help you at all?' 'No! Thank you. Please, leave it. I've got to do this on my own.' Philip was a lovely man. I couldn't do his lunch justice., 'You don't eat much!' he said. 'I have never been a big eater. This is more than I have eaten in a long while, and I have enjoyed it. Thank you.' We walked some more. Philip was a very interesting man to be with, pointing out different places of interest.

In that year we did so much. I remember; Vixen Tor, Brent Tor, Princetown, Two Bridges, Horrabridge, Sheepstor, Widecombe, Buckland in the Moor, Post Bridge, Haytor, Abbots Way, The Old Railway, and a lot of other places. There is another place we went to. It was creepy and so cold, even on a lovely summer's day, it was called Wistman's Wood. Most Wednesdays, Philip saw his friends and I saw Mable.

One time, coming back from the moors we stopped off at Philip's bungalow, a nice place. The garden was big and so lovely that I fell in love with it. But it needed a lot of work. Philip couldn't get over the interest I showed in his garden. I started to say, 'If this was my place, I would have a pond in this spot, with water lilies and irises here, as they like the damp.' 'That would be a good idea, Faith.' 'Over here, where you have really neglected this spot, I suggest we could clear a path through the trees, and plant snowdrops, crocuses, bluebells, foxgloves, those kinds of things. We could call it The Glade. What do you think?'

I turned around, to see his face beaming. 'Oh, I got carried, away, didn't I?' His face was still beaming, and he just hugged me. 'You are the only one that ever took an interest in my garden. I like your ideas. Will you help me with my garden?' 'You don't need to ask me,' I replied. 'After all you have done for me helping me to plant all those lovely veggies, why can't I help you with yours? While you have been taking me out and doing things for me you have been neglecting your own garden.' So, we started to work to tidy his garden. It was almost October. We did enjoy each other's company and were so happy together. Philip had most of his meals at my place, so he kept the pantry well stocked. He wouldn't let me pay for anything. He dropped me to work every night, and we worked between his place and mine. Maude loved him. When we were working in our garden, she would be down, with the tea. They would be off talking about the old days. They had been born in the same year, with Union Street dividing them, both living at either end.

One day, Maude asked me if there was anything in the air. 'What do you mean?' 'You know, Philip and you?' 'We are just good friends. He lives in his house and I live in mine. We just like each other's company, and we help each other out. He is still missing his wife; I cook for him and Philip does a lot of work for me; things that need doing around my flat. Our pastimes are walking, birdwatching, music, and gardening. That's all, at the moment, Maude!' One day I got up about four. Philip was outside in the garden. I made him a cup of tea and started to cook the dinner.

Philip loved his food, and most of all, my cooking. Then he would take me to work. He was such a dear. He was saving me a lot of money, and my debts were reducing quickly. With all the jobs Philip was doing he wouldn't take a penny from me. He said my company gave him great pleasure. I was able to drop a night, and I was not filling in at work so much. So, now I was only doing fifty-five hours a week. Philip was very pleased because it meant we had more time together.

Christmas had come and gone. It was January 1998. Rosie, David, and the children, had met Philip. They all seemed to like him very much. In March of that year, he gave me a ring, but he only called it a friendship ring. I think Philip was beginning to recover from his grief of losing his wife. But, like me, we were not ready to make a commitment. He lived in his home and I lived in mine. Sometime around Easter, the grandchildren came down for a holiday. I don't remember if we stayed with Philip, or if he picked us up, from my place. I remembered us all going to the beach; Geo was about two and would always want to be with Philip. There was an awful moment when Philip had gone over the rocks to see what was over the other side and I was getting the picnic out. The children were playing. When I looked up, Geo was halfway up the rocks. We all shouted to Philip, 'Geo is following you.' Philip told him to stay where he was and brought him safely down. The children adored Philip.

45

At the end of June 1998, I went to a well woman clinic. She took blood and did a smear test, then examined my breast. 'You have got a lump here which could be cancer.' All I could see was my brother in his bed, a bag of bones. Was this going to be how I would end? The doctor said, 'You have got a lump in your left breast so you need to go to Derriford Hospital for a biopsy. You will hear in the next few days.' Which I did. 'Do you want to know the results of your biopsy? I said 'Yes, Please.' There was someone in a white coat, it could have been a doctor, but it was a nurse doing all the talking., 'It's going to hurt,' the nurse said, 'Keep as still as you can,' as he plunged this long needle into me, and drew out some fluid. Hurt! That was an understatement. The nurse held my hand all the time to comfort me. She was lovely and gave my hand a little squeeze now and again.

Philip was waiting for me and I went back and joined him in the waiting room. In about half an hour the nurse came out and we were ushered into another room. She nodded for Philip to come with us. The doctor said, 'About your biopsy. You want it straight?' I nodded. Philip put out his hand to hold mine. We both knew what was coming. Then the doctor told us it was cancer. I was dumbfounded. My thoughts went back to my brother again when he had died of cancer. The doctor was telling me I needed an operation. 'You should hear soon.' Philip took me home. I was stunned. 'Would you like me to stay?' he asked. 'No. I will be alright. I have got to face it.' We said good night.

Maude heard Philip drive away in his car, and she came down to me. 'How did things go?' 'Not good. Cancer. Philip wanted to stay with me tonight which was dear of him, but tomorrow I have got to tell him he must leave me. I can't put him through this again.' It was just under two years since he lost his wife. 'What if I don't make it?' Maude said, 'He won't leave. You don't see what I see when he is around you. You're still wrapped up in your own hurt. Not all men are the same, Faith. If am a good judge of character, he won't leave you.'

We had a cup of tea. 'I don't want him to leave me, Maude. But I have got to give him the easy way out. I owe it to him.'

The next day Philip was down by ten o'clock. I gave him back his ring. 'I don't know what is in store for me, if I will live or die. This is a journey I must take on my own. Philip said, 'You can put that ring back on again! And I will be putting another one on that finger as soon as I can! Today, after our cup of tea, you are going up to your workplace to hand in your notice. Then we are going to the furniture shop and pick out some furniture for your bedroom. In the meantime, I will do up the spare room. When you come out of hospital, you are coming home with me. That will be your home, as we are going to get married.'

I had the operation in July 1998. They just cut out the lump and two lymph nodes. A week after, I had to go to the oncology clinic. I was told they had found more cancer. This meant another operation, to remove all the lymph nodes from under the left arm. I was back in hospital again at the end of July 1998. Two operations in one month. In a few days, I was back with Philip in my lovely new bedroom which Philip and I would soon share. This now was my home. In a few days, things were going wrong for me. Cellulitis set in which rotted the skin. The stitches fell out and I was left with this open wound with smelly body fluid leaking out. The hole was big enough to put my fist in, and was very, very painful. Philip took me down to the hospital to see my nurse.

You are allotted a nurse for your after care. As soon as she saw me, she called the doctor in. The doctor prescribed me antibiotics. It took three lots of very strong antibiotics to clear it. Once you have had all your lymph nodes removed from under your armpit you have got no immunity in that part of the body. The nurse got me some boob tubes and padded me up. She said I could use sanitary towels to soak up the fluid. It was a mess. And to top it all, I had to exercise the left arm twice a day, by walking my fingers up the wall. It was so painful. I couldn't stop crying. But, to get another finger higher was jubilation. It was a long slog before I could get my arm above my head again. But I did it. I got there. I felt so pleased with myself.

One day when I first started my exercises, when it was so very painful, I was still crying when the phone went. It was my sister Peggy. Her first words were, 'What are you snivelling about?' 'I have just been doing my exercises, and it was very painful.' 'Oh, that is nothing!' she retorted. 'I put my back out yesterday, lifting a lady.' I said, 'Sorry,' and put down the phone. To me it was like an icy blast from the past. I could hear Mum saying it, 'Peggy is ill; not you,' and I waited for the smack across my ear. It was not just physical pain I was going through, it was also mental, wondering if this hole under my arm would ever close over. I was not looking for sympathy. But now I couldn't stop crying. I was in so much pain, so much discomfort, and this horrible smelly fluid. It was all too much for me right then.

Philip came in and put his arm gently around me. 'What's upset you, Love?' I told him what Peggy had said, and how I felt the blast from the past. 'Whatever is the matter with that woman?' he exclaimed. 'It's not Peggy's fault,' I said, 'It is the words Mum put into her head; she brained-washed us both and as a result Peggy will always be more poorly than me. She soon learned to put on the agony. Philip said, 'No, I disagree, because as much as you try to hide it from me, I can see you are in a lot of pain. It is demoralising for you, Love. I think that big open wound I dress most days is frightening you because you think it won't heal up.' Philip was right. I had learned to cover up my hurt feelings from a very early age. You must smile to hide your pain. Very few people can see through me.

46

I felt at that moment God was smiling down at me. He had sent this loving man to care for me in my time of need. Philip was so loving and caring. Peggy didn't phone for a while. The hole gradually closed, and I could lift my arm much more easily. I had to see the doctor at the oncology department to talk about having chemotherapy. Philip came with me to the doctor, who told us all about chemo, that if I had it, I stood 90% chance of a full recovery. Would I agree to have it? I said yes!

Then Philip said to the doctor, 'How soon can we get married?' 'Right away, before she starts chemo!' the doctor said, 'It will do her good!' We could get married on the sixteenth of September 1998. 'Are you going away?' the doctor asked. 'No, I don't think Faith is ready for that at the moment,' said Philip. They said all of this as if I wasn't there. I was looking from the doctor and Philip in amazement because we never even talked about it! I remember Philip saying at the first opportunity, 'We will marry!' Then the doctor said to Philip, 'The sooner the better. We will start the treatment for her chemo on the 18th of September.

There were only to be the two of us, and two witnesses, at the wedding. But the moment I phoned my two daughters to tell them, they said, 'You can't get married without us!' So, I ended up with two lovely bridesmaids and a pageboy. Lydia came around and made my dress practically overnight. Viv phoned up to see how I was getting on. I told them. They both came along, and her husband took the photos. So much for a quiet wedding! Philip and I went to Tesco, and got pasties, sausage rolls and other goodies. The wedding went off beautifully and everyone came back to the bungalow. My two girls couldn't thank Philip enough for looking after me so well.

Philip really took to my grandchildren, as it was granddad this, and granddad that. The grandchildren took to Philip right away, and he loved them, and my daughters. 'By marrying one woman, I have ended up with a beautiful wife and a lovely family; what more can a man wish for?' You could see he was so happy. Every opportunity, after the chemo, we would have the children down in their holidays.

'I start chemo from the 18th of September, and will be on chemo for six months,' I told my girls. The next six months were hard. There were so many side effects with me feeling ill most of the time. And blood transfusions, too. Then in and out of hospital. So many things went wrong. I was sitting up in bed one day, feeling rather sorry for myself, because I couldn't sleep, and suddenly it felt as if someone sad down on the bed bedside me. I turned my head and there was my dear Gran Richards. She parted my fringe. Then I felt her lips kissing my forehead as she had done many times before. 'Everything is going to be alright, Faith,' she said, before standing up and starting to walk towards the corner of the room. I shouted, 'Don't go, Granny,' and I felt tears well up as she disappeared in a grey mist. Philip woke up. 'Why are you crying, Love?' 'Granny's gone,' I said. He put his arms around me.

My immunity system had broken down completely. The doctor said later that he didn't know where to start as I had so many problems at once. First was to bring down my temperature, which had hit the roof. I was on the bed in just a very thin nightie, with a huge great fan blowing cold air at me. I was in and out of sleep all the time. I remember waking up once, shivering and asking why they were punishing me, saying I haven't done anything wrong. Could I have a blanket? I was so cold. The nurses finally got my temperature down and said, 'You can have your blanket now!' They were laughing at me. 'Did I say what I think?' I asked. 'Yes!' she said, still laughing. Next, the doctor needed to get antibiotics in fast. They were administered intravenously, and after that, another blood transfusion.

The doctor came over, 'We won in the end, but I never saw so many bugs in one person,' he said. 'Do you mind if I bring a young lady over in her bed bedside you? She needs a blood transfusion, and she is very much afraid. If she watches the procedure with you, she might be persuaded.' I said it was alright. They brought her over in her bed, and she watched me. My drip was set up. She asked me if it hurt. I was honest, 'Just a little, as the needle goes in. Just clench your teeth, that's all I do.' 'You didn't even blink!' she exclaimed. She called the nurse over, 'Set me up, please. If *she* can take it, I can too.' We laid in

165

our beds talking. The doctor did a thumbs up to us. 'He is a lovely doctor.' I said, 'It is time we had a little nap; this always make me sleepy.' After that, I was allowed home.

Philip was so pleased to see me. But it was short lived. I was soon back in hospital again with more side effects. This time it was deep vein thrombosis but again they sorted me out. I was put on warfarin for the next six months, and I was sent home. Once more, Peggy phoned and asked where I had been. I made light of it. I said, 'Oh, I got a bad leg thrombosis.' 'Oh,' Peggy said. 'I went to the doctor today. He told me I've got a touch of thrombosis, and he told me to keep my weight off it.' I thought, 'Peggy, why don't you grow up? You can't get *a TOUCH OF THROMBOSIS!*' I wanted to put the phone down on her. If only she knew how dangerous it was. Deep vein thrombosis was a clot of blood which, if not treated with warfarin, could travel up to the heart, or lungs, or head, and kill you. As it did to my son, Paul, just a year ago in 2018.

Peggy went on to say, 'Can I come down for the weekend?' I looked at Philip. He said yes, despite not liking her much because of the way she treated me. Philip was building a built-in-wardrobe in the other room, for when the children came down. He had the drawers on the bed to make the furniture lighter to move. I noticed his drawers were nice and neat, just as he was. All his private papers were in one, and in another, was his dead wife's funeral plan. He put them back in the chest, so that Peggy could sleep in the room. When she arrived, we took her out and about. She was awful. She tried to tell Philip what to watch on telly, but Philip told her that he didn't watch soaps. 'There is a telly in your bedroom. Watch your soaps there and don't expect Faith to wait on you hand and foot,' he said.

I told Peggy dinner was ready. She told me she didn't eat a lot as she couldn't swallow, so I put a little potato on her plate. 'Is this enough for you?' 'Oh, yes.' She ate a little of it. 'Oh! Cheesy potatoes!' and she went back to the saucepan and took nearly all of the rest. 'What are you doing?' I said, 'that's Philip's and mine.' She just walked out of the kitchen. I turned around and made some more and brought in Philip's and my dinner. When Peggy came back in, she started to speak. 'I am going to retire soon so Tim and I can come down for three months at a time which would be nice! You could drive us out on the moor and Tim and I could sit outside the car with our cups of tea while you do your walking. By the way, Philip, my train leaves North Road at ten thirty.' She was just going to say, 'I need you to….,' but I stopped her before she finished the sentence. 'Philip's got something to do. We are going to get the bus instead.' I had got fed up with her using us.

When I came home, Philip was in the green house. 'Do you want me to help to pick out these seedlings, or do you want to get on with the bedroom?' Philip said, 'We'll do the bedroom. I could finish that job today.' 'I will cook lunch. Shall we have it outside since it is such a lovely day?' 'Yes please, Love,' Philip replied. We ate our lunch and talked about how bossy Peggy was. I told you this before. You can only stand her in small doses. She takes over your life. 'And as for her and Tim staying here for three months, she can think again; I am not keeping them for three months. She will go home and blow it on bingo. No way!'

Philip started to laugh. 'It sounds as if you don't like your sister!' I said, 'No… I don't like her ways. But I love her because she is my sister. I will do the dishes later. I will come in and sit on the bed just in case you want a hand.' Philip started to take the drawers out so that he could move the furniture, and what we saw upset us. The funeral plan was in disarray and bottom side up. She had not left one drawer untouched. Philip turned to me. 'I am not getting at you, Faith but I don't want your sister here ever again. Her behaviour is diabolical. She might be your sister, but she has gone too far this time.' He walked out of the room; he was really upset. She had gone through all his private papers. What right did she have to do it? What kind of person was she?

47

I finished chemotherapy. I started to feel better now, but I now had to go on a course of radiotherapy. That was March 1999. Twenty-two days, for ten minutes each day, with those big machines being lowered so near to your body was very frightening. After that course, I had to have a lot of tests to make sure the cancer had not spread. Because the cancer had spread to my lymph nodes, I needed a nuclear bone scan in 2000. Then I needed an MRI scan, because I was getting trouble with my back. It turned out that my lower lumber region had collapsed and I was now nearly four inches shorter. No more being six foot in my high heel shoes. The doctor was not happy. So, three months later I had another MRI. I was clear of cancer at last. The doctor and nursing staff looked after me so well. And so did my Philip. He had come to every appointment and visited me every day I was in hospital. He nursed me all the way through my illness. When I was not feeling well, he was just there for me. He was so loving and tender. He was a darling. At last, I had a husband in a million. How many women can say that? Even when I was a pretty awful sight, what with that great big hole under my arm pit which Philip helped to tend to; and being so sick while I was on the chemo. He was always there for me. I feel that I have been blessed.

On my good days I would help around the garden, pulling a few weeds, or picking out seedlings. I was doing more and more each day. Even doing a lot more home cooking. Philip loved my homemade pasties! We started to go for short walks on the moors, going farther each time and we were bird watching again. I took him to Slapton Ley. 'I did not realise that there was so much bird life here,' Philip said. 'But now I am going to treat *you* to the best fish and chips, in the south west. It's Torcross Pub. This place is steeped in history. See that tank across the way? I have heard two different stories to this. One of them was that the Americans were doing manoeuvres around this coast when everything went drastically wrong. A lot of the American troops died that day. That tank was bought up from the seabed and set as a tribute to all the Americans who lost their lives. God bless them.'

We started to have the grandchildren down a lot more when they were on their holidays, which helped Rosie and David a lot. One day, Rosie told me that she and David had left their three children to be brought up by me in their will if anything should happen to the them. What a tribute to me. I could have wept for joy that they could put such a trust in me. But God had other plans, that Rosie should be here for me. Philip loved having the children down. He had swings and climbing nets hanging from the trees. To be honest with you, I don't know who the biggest kid was! If we went to the beach, we would end up having water fights, throwing buckets of water over each other. It was lovely having the grandchildren. They made us feel so young and we all had the time of our lives.

Rosie and David took Philip, me and the children down the Solent in their yacht and we saw the tall ships. That was a lovely day out. The next day, we went to France on the hovercraft to visit the Normandy beaches. We spent a couple of days exploring around that area. It was very interesting and a lovely time to remember. The following year we went to France having rented a big gite, hoping all the family would join us. No luck. We had a lovely time anyway. Coming back from Roscoff on the ferry, we suffered a force nine gale. Rosie gave us each a pill and we all went to sleep and didn't wake up until we got to Plymouth.

The children loved my cooking. Sometimes, they liked to help me. I would ask them what they would like and very often they would say stew, even in the middle of summer. I would do it for them if that's what they wanted. If I cooked something like corned beef hash, all four squabbled over all the crispy bits left on the side of the cooking dish. I told them that by the time they had finished scraping the dish out, there would be no need to wash it, because they would have licked it clean. They laughed, and there was a big grin on Philip's face. It was nice to see Philip with the children; he really enjoyed having them down.

Philip was a good artist. He loved to help the two girls, and showed them how, by shading their pictures, it would come alive. They would spend hours doing this when it was raining. We had colouring books for Geo, as he was a bit young at that time. He was such a dear. He did so love his Granddad. Philip said he loved having

169

the grandchildren down and would miss them when they went back. 'There is always another school holiday, Love, but I think you will miss the pillow fights in the morning!' Philip laughed and said, 'You were right on that first day we met, Faith; that children can be a blessing. My children have been a blessing in my life. They are everything to live for. I love them so much, even though it is hard work sometimes, wondering if you are making the right decisions for them. But it is all worthwhile in the end.'

I had to go to the Lymphoedema clinic because of my left arm. It was badly swollen, and I had to wear a compression sleeve. It was always so painful, and still is. I mustn't carry heavy weights and I have got to be very careful at all times; no blood pressure, no needles to take blood, no injections. It left the arm very weak, with no strength in it at all, and no immunity. When I went out with Mable, I would look around the shops and buy the children clothes. When it was raining, we would have a fashion show. It was a bit of a giggle! They had to pretend they were on the catwalk. I would describe the outfits they had on, and Philip would make a video of them. I would put them on a DVD so that they can have them later in life.

Philip was so amiable; you couldn't fall out with him. He would say, 'We all can't think alike!' It was so relaxing being with him. We enjoyed our time together. He took me to Spain a lot, but I especially loved it when we went to Malta because there was so much to see.

48

In 2005 it was Paul's fiftieth birthday. We asked all the family down and we gave him a party. Lydia made the cake. We all had a good time, but no Robin. He didn't turn up until we were about to pack up but he was invited to spend the weekend. We gave him a room to share with Paul, hoping they would catch up as they hadn't seen each other for a long time.

Philip tried to speak to Robin, but Robin was so rude to him. I don't know what was said, but Philip was going to offer Robin a home with us if he got too ill to work. Philip said, 'I would have done this for you, Faith. I know how much you worried about him. But not now, Faith. Not after this.' Philip was really hurt. I asked Lydia and Jake to drop Robin off to his hotel, as there were no buses.

On the way back Lydia said, 'Why are you so awful to Mum, Robin?' 'Because she took everything away from Ed. You have been back to the house to collect your things. Who had the house, the furniture, and the car?' 'Mum only took all the presents she was given over the years, some pots and pan and sheets, blankets and towels. That is all she took from there. Also, the smaller of the two endowments they had, so that she was able to buy her flat. I was there; I helped her.' Robin said, 'Where did she get her money from to put furniture in the flat?' 'Mum worked very hard for it. She put it on her credit card; then she had to pay it back. I know she even paid back the thousand pounds Ed owed you for the car, because you queried one of the payments when she was so sick. I had to go through them. Ed refused to pay it and Mum did it as she felt it was a part of her debt. But Mum never went out with other men. She had to work all hours to pay off the debts that Ed kept running up. That is, until her health started to fail her because of the mental cruelty he was putting her through. And Ed and his daughter were going to throw Mum out on the street, until I stepped in.'

Lydia continued, 'Mum met Philip in November 1996, eleven months after her divorce, at the station, as she was on the way up to see Rosie. Up until then Ed was always on the scene. They even went out together on a Sunday. It was from the New Year party 1997 that Mum would not take Ed back. That is when Ed started to blacken both Philip and Mum's names. Now his daughter's got everything she wanted. She never bothered about her father.'

The last time I was in hospital was in 2007. It was just after Lydia had her heart attack, at the age of forty-nine. I blamed Lydia for giving me such a fright. I had shingles, first in the head, then all over the body. I still never had chickenpox. Having shingles in the head was most painful; I couldn't stop screaming. The pain was worse than childbirth. I was in hospital for six weeks. The doctor wouldn't let me home until they had done all the tests, as they thought I had had a stroke as well as I had no feeling in the bottom of my feet. I still haven't got much feeling there. It's the same in my fingertips.

They kept me hanging around. I asked if I could come in as an outpatient. The doctor didn't want that. 'Well, I will sign myself out, as I can see my husband is so very ill and needs me home, so that I can care for him.' All through those six weeks, Rosie was there for us every weekend. She would come down from Southampton, do the shopping for Philip, do our washing, making sure I had everything I needed. She was lovely, and so reliable. I don't know what we would have done without her. The doctor said, 'Give us two more days. We need to do a little operation behind the ear to see if the blood is flowing to the brain and then another MRI scan. Then you can go home.' I was relieved. The doctors never sent for me or sent any correspondence, but there couldn't have been anything else wrong as I am still alive and kicking. Philip was very pleased to see me home.

I finally got Philip to see the doctor. I was so worried about him, but it was an uphill job. We both went in to see the doctor. It was a good job I did as Philip was making light of things. I stepped in, 'Please, doctor listen to me as Philip is having some kind of turns and no two are the same.' I explained some of the symptoms. The doctor said, 'He needs to go hospital for a cat scan.' His general health had also deteriorated. After the doctor examined Philip he said, 'I am going to send you to the prostate clinic.'

Looking at Philip the doctor said, 'You are going to receive appointments through the post.' It's the only time I saw Philip angry with me and he kept it up for a few days. I didn't take it to heart. I know he didn't like going to the doctors or hospitals, but I was much happier now that I had set the ball rolling. Philip soon said, 'Sorry, Puppy.' This was one of his terms of endearments for me! He said I was so cuddly! I said, 'I am sorry too, but I did need to step in. It is my turn to look after you now, so please let me do it. I love you and want you around.' It did turn out to be prostate cancer. Philip had had it for a long time, and it had seeped into his bones, for which he was having treatment and a cat scan. It turned out he was having fits, which the hospital was going to keep an eye on.

Philip bought me a second-hand car. It was an automatic car, as I was finding it hard to change the gears with my left arm. So, I could do all the driving from now on. I bought Philip a very light-weight wheelchair. He kicked up a fuss about this, but I said, 'There is no use you kicking up a fuss. You can't walk the long hospital corridors and I can't push those heavy wheelchairs in the hospital. We have got to work together. I am a lot stronger now. I know there are still a lot of things I can't do, but I do know my limits.' I took him shopping and I took him to the edge of the moors for picnics. He really loved that. Some days we would just sit in the garden. He had come to terms with his illness.

49

In 2008, I started to get problems with my breathing. I went to the doctor and told her about my breathing difficulties. They did an ECG. 'We need to send you to heart foundation clinic. It is the next turning, just after Derriford Hospital. You will be sent an appointment.' I got the appointment. It was a lovely day, so I walked down. When I got there, they took another E.C.G. They stuck some pads on me, then put a belt with a small black box on it and plugged in the wires from the pads. I had to wear this for twenty-four hours and come back the same time the following day. They took the pads and the belt off, then I had to wait for the technician to come back. 'You have an irregular heartbeat,' was the response. 'I need you to take tablets for it.' I needed to play this down a bit, or Philip wouldn't have let me help. By this time, he needed help to walk across the sitting room. It was so pitiful for me to watch this man who used to walk ten to twelve miles a day, across rough terrain, with a backpack on his back, right up until his early eighties. Now, he could not walk across the sitting room. I had to help him wash and dress him.

It was now 2010. Rosie came down with my grandson, Geo, and the two dogs for the weekend. Rosie, having the bigger car, did the driving so we went out on the moors. As soon as we got there, something peculiar happened. Instead of the dogs running off with Geo, Philip sat down on his seat with the dogs, one either side of him. There was a stillness, a silence. Even Geo, a couple of steps in front of Rosie, had stopped. It was a beautiful sunny day in February. Philip had tears running down his cheeks. He reached down to pet the dogs and not a word was said between the four of us. I would like to think he was remembering the happy times we all spent on the moors. It was as if we were all spellbound and we stood like statues. Then Philip said he was cold and wanted to go back to the car. We had all spent a lovely weekend together.

Rosie, Geo and the dogs went back. Philip made me promise, 'I know you will downsize when I go, and you will get good money for this property. So, when you have bought your flat and all the things you will need in it, I want you to give the remainder of the money from the sale of the property, to Rosie. It can help to send those lovely grandchildren to university. Plus, when *you* go, Rosie must have that big sapphire ring. This is to thank her for her kindness over the years.'

Philip was going to bed early, about seven every evening. It was the 5th of March 2010. Every evening I would sit on the bed while he watched T.V. I would work on my laptop, maybe putting fresh music on his M.P.3. player, or sorting photos or sometimes just playing games. I was happy just being bedside him. If it gave him comfort by my being there, what more could I ask for? Philip was such a loving man. He was always there for me. Philip had gone to sleep, and I was watching a film. It was about eleven o'clock. He started to make a noise in his throat. I gave him a shake and called his name, but he did not wake. I tried to put him on his side, but no luck, so I called 999.

Someone at the other end asked if I needed the police or ambulance. I said, 'Ambulance, please.' They put me right through. They asked me my name and address then what was wrong. 'My husband,' I said. 'He's making an awful noise in his throat. What was going through my head was this was what people call the death rattle. I can't wake him or turn him on his side. I have tried.' The voice on the other end of the phone said, 'The ambulance will be with you soon. I will stay on the phone with you all the time. Don't unlock the door until I tell you. What is your husband doing now? Is it very much the same?' I put the phone over to Philip, so she could hear the noise. She asked, 'Has your husband had any illness lately?' 'Yes, he has got prostate cancer and is also fitting, that's why I tried to turn him on his side, just in case he was going to be sick. But I have only got one good arm, so I am finding him too heavy for me.' 'It won't be long now. The ambulance is nearly there. Just stay on the phone. I will tell you when,' and she chatted away. It was such a comfort to know you were not on your own. I sat on the bed, holding my Philip's hand.

At last she said, 'Open the door.' I let the ambulance personnel in. They went right over to my Philip. The lady told me to dress as they were taking Philip into hospital. I picked up my handbag and coat and locked the front door. They put Philip in the ambulance, but I had to sit in the front with the lady driver. I could hear them in the back of the ambulance trying to bring Philip around. We soon got to the hospital A&E as it was only a stone's throw away from our house. Philip was wheeled away, down the corridor. I was shown into a little room. A nurse brought me a cup of tea. The nurse said, 'Is there anyone you need to call?' 'Yes please, if I may. My daughter!' 'There's a pay phone over there.' I called Lydia, 'What is it, Mum?' 'Philip! We are in A&E.' I told her briefly all I knew. 'We will be right there!' said Lydia. It was lovely to have someone with me.

Shortly after, a doctor came in. She told us, 'Your husband has had a stroke and was fitting. We don't expect him to pull through. The doctor took us to Philip. He was in a bed with the sides up. Lydia's husband said, 'Shall we have someone in to read his last rites?' 'Yes please,' I said. And that was done. We sat there a little longer and we saw a movement under the blanket. 'He is mumbling something like Poppy,' Lydia said. My face lit up. 'No! That's one of his endearments for me, Puppy!' I gave his hand a squeeze. 'Where am I?' he asked. 'In hospital, Love; you have had a stroke.' I suggested Lydia and Jake said their goodbyes and went home to get some more shuteye. 'Will you be so kind as to come back later this morning? And Lydia, will you sit with Philip so that Jake can take me home, so that I can wash and change and have something to eat. I would be very grateful.' 'Yes,' they both said.

Philip was going in and out of sleep. As I sat quietly, the nurse came in and told me they were going to move Philip up to a ward. I told Lydia this when she came back. 'Will you let me know if I am at home?' 'Yes, Mum.' She phoned me just as I was about to leave the bungalow and Lydia told me where Philip had been moved to. She said Philip would be in a ward by the time I got back. I sat at his bedside. Both of us were going in and out of sleep. People came to see us throughout the day, asking questions. One was the welfare lady, asking whether we would need any kind of help. 'Yes, to find us a new home! I can't manage that big garden.' Philip smiled. He agreed. 'We must think about it. It's early days yet and it all depends what Philip is like when he comes home. I walked to the door with the lady. I told her that I knew it depended on how much the stroke and the fits had affected Philip.

One of the nurses came over to tell me Philip was going to be moved upstairs to the stroke ward. 'The doctor will be over to see you soon.' Lydia came in again, then the doctor came over. He turned to Philip and asked how he was doing. Philip just nodded. The doctor turned to me again. 'When we move him upstairs, we will be able to see how movement has been affected and we can work from there.' When they left us, I said to Lydia, 'Will you please sit with Philip while I go up to the stroke ward?' I went to ask the nurse at the desk the name of the stroke ward and how to get there.

I went up and saw the duty nurse on the ward. I told her my husband was coming up later and asked if there was any way I could help, like washing him or feeding him because I had been a carer. 'Yes, I would like you to come and help,' she said. 'We are overworked.' 'What time do you want me?' 'About nine!' 'That will be lovely.' I went back to Philip and Lydia. I had to leave. I kissed Philip goodbye and said goodbye to Lydia and went home to an empty bungalow. I made myself something to eat, sat down in the lounge and looked at Philip's empty seat. I had never felt so lonely in my life as I did right then. So, I went to bed and slept. The phone rang. It was two o'clock in the morning on the 6th of March 2010. I answered the phone. 'Your husband is not expected to last long. Please come in right away.'

I phoned Lydia, asking her to pick me up as Philip was dying. 'I've been called in. Will you come with me, please?' They picked me up and took me in. But he had just passed away. I remember screaming at Philip, 'Why did you have to go and leave me?' Philip was at peace now. I kissed him. He was still warm. I said, 'Let's go. He isn't here.' At home, while Lydia was saying her goodbyes, all I could think of was that last smile and that look of love, just for me, as I left the day before. Now, my heart was breaking. I will never ever feel his loving arms around me again. God had blessed me and given me this wonderful man. 'Thank you, God.'

50

Lydia and hubby stayed with me the rest of the night. They started going through some of his papers. My marriage certificate and some of my private papers were all thrown in a box, so I phoned Rosie and David. Rosie said that the first thing to do was to see Philip's solicitor, as Philip's executor, to find out what she needed and how to go about probate. Then we started to go through Philip's papers. David was back and forward to the tip for a week. It did poor David in, as he was working so hard. Paul was getting things down from the loft and putting it in the garden. You never seen so much rubbish in your life. To Philip it 'might come in handy one day,' even down to a piece of string about six inches long. He was a magpie.

I helped Rosie sort a lot of the paperwork out. I had to open drawers and cupboards I had never been in; in all the time I had lived there. I felt it was an invasion of his privacy even now as I was doing it. Rosie and I had been up to one o'clock that morning, looking through these papers. Most of it was to do with his previous wife. Lydia came in, 'What have you been doing going through the paper? She was an executor as well. 'Where and what have you thrown away?' Rosie said, 'Out in the dustbin.' Lydia stomped out and brought back the black bags and threw it all over the living floor. 'This was all to do with Philip's previous wife, some of her clothes and old papers that should have been thrown out years ago. They are nothing to do with Philip.' Now, I don't know what happened. I was screaming, shouting and stamping my feet, crying like I was a mad woman. It was hard enough going through it all once, but to see it all over the floor again, was too much. I flipped my lid.

Another time Lydia came up with the same kind of attitude. 'I have come up to inspect your boundary,' she announced. She did and found there was nothing wrong with the boundary. Then, all of a sudden, she turned on me, 'You need to tidy this garden up!' I told her, 'I've got one pair hands and Paul has as well. We have been working flat out for nearly a month. It is the end of March and it has been raining heavy lately. If you were a gardener, you would know you don't work on wet soil.

We put the bungalow on the market. It was sold in three days, but they couldn't move into it until August, as we had to wait until probate went through. With other different legal things, Philip had left me very comfortably off. God must have been smiling on me to find a lovely flat for sale, here in my beloved Teignmouth, not far from where I grew up. Probate was to take place in Philip's bank on the 13th of August. Philip's money was to be paid over to me. But Rosie and Lydia had to be there to sign for it. This date had been prearranged a while back, but Jake phoned Rosie the day before and said that Lydia would not be there, as they were going out and that Rosie had no business organising their lives. Apparently, it was very heated, and Rosie was very upset. Anyway, Lydia did turn up to sign. It took about ten minutes and she was gone. Rosie met me in my bank, and we sent off the money to pay for my flat and any another money that needed to be paid at that time.

I left Plymouth on the 14th of August 2010. I was 75 now and in three months' time I would be 76. Since my flat was not ready to move into yet I stayed with Peggy and Tim for five weeks. I bought most of the food for us and other things they needed as Peggy wouldn't take keep from me as they were on benefits. When Tim went into a nursing home, I gave Peggy half towards new carpet throughout the whole of her flat, plus a new cleaner, just to say thank you. I was very grateful. After five weeks I moved into my new flat. It was lovely.

I soon got into a routine. The Alice Cross on Monday; singing on Tuesday; line dancing on Wednesday. Later, I joined the Women's Fellowship at the Baptist Church. I soon made friends. I would go to films and shows, tea dances up the Alice Cross. One of my friends talked me into joining the choir Teignmouth Sings. I really enjoyed this as I love to sing. I also took part in shows at the Alice Cross. I started to have quite a full life. Plus, my children and grandchildren would come to see me. Sometimes they would stay for a few days, sometimes longer. I would go on holiday with the children. I also took Peggy on holiday. She was never left out.

My sister April was very ill now. I had her down on two occasions. She was full of love and happiness although she was dying. I love my April. The bond between us never broke. I love her so much and I knew she loved me; I had no doubts about it. We laughed and sang together. Even walking along, pushing April in the wheelchair, we would be singing! We got some very strange looks, but we went on singing. We were happy together. I would have loved to nurse her until the end, but my health started to deteriorate.

Each time April was down we saw very little of Peggy. I don't know why. She only lived across the road. After April went back the second time, April said that Peggy had phoned her. She was in tears, saying I had changed towards her, and accusing April of taking me away. How childish can you get? I could not push April up the hill to Peggy's as she was too heavy for me. Each time we went up the Alice Cross, I had to have a taxi. In the end, April went into a nursing home. I would see my April most weekends. My nieces or nephews would take me to see her. I would always ask if there was enough room in the car for Peggy, just in case she wanted to come and see her sister. Peggy only came the once, when our nephew took us. Roughly about this time is when she told me she wouldn't go to April's funeral. I told her, 'If that's how you feel, but we will cross that bridge when the time comes.'

Then I went down with bronchitis and was ill for about three weeks. I never saw Peggy in all the time I was ill. Rosie said we should go on our holiday as planned as she would be there to look after me. We had a nice holiday. I was also going to stay with my Rosie and Zoe, my granddaughter, for a week. Since there was not enough room in the house, Zoe and I slept in the caravan. In the morning we were both ill, so Rosie put us in the car, took me home and called the doctor in for me. I had a bad chest infection.

Rosie got my prescription which was for antibiotics and made sure I had enough food. You could see Rosie didn't want to leave me. I told her to get Zoe back to her doctor. She made sure I had everything I needed and then she took Zoe back to Reading. From there, she had to go back to Southampton, as she had to be at work the next day.

While I was so ill, I had a phone call from my niece saying that April's life was coming to an end. The antibiotics I was on were serving me badly. There was no way I could go to my April and hold her hand and say my goodbyes. My April died on the 13th April 2012, at the age of 79. My niece took me up to the funeral parlour to say my goodbyes to her. She looked so peaceful now, dressed in her lilac satin. I held her hand as I bent over to kiss her and told her I would miss her. 'Goodbye, my lovely sister.' I pray to God to take care of her soul for me.

I wouldn't be attending the funeral, so my Rosie stepped in for me. It clashed with the little holiday I had planned for Paul's birthday, to visit some of the war graves in France. He wanted to do this as he wanted to visit some of the plots of our fallen relations in the First World War. We found some of our family names on graves and memorials in France. Then we went on to Brussels. At the memorial at the Menin-Gate, we found more family.

When we came back, it was arranged to do a Memorial for April. I took the family around to some of the places April and I had played as children. At each place I said a little prayer for her. I felt her so near. And we left a handful of her ashes in the places. We played first by the quay, where we swam as children. How we loved to play here in the water. Then I put a handful outside Grannie's house. I said, 'We can't forget our lovely Gran, can we?' Then from there we went by the pier. I went by the water's edge where we would swim, putting a handful there too. 'You are at peace now, my darling sister. All I can do is to remember the happy times we spent together, swimming, running, playing, cycling and the love you gave to me. I wish I could hold your hand now and run up the beach together. Goodbye, my darling.' Sweet, sweet memories. I took all the family for a meal in the evening, then the next day my niece took me to April's village Church. Her ashes were blessed and put in the ground.

51

It had been a long time since I had seen Peggy. I started to worry. It looked as if she was in one of her moods again. They were always so petty. So, I tried phoning her. But she had one of these phones where you could see who was phoning, so she never answered me. I didn't know what to do. But, while I was having my hair done, my hairdresser asked me what I was looking so worried about. 'Oh, I was thinking about my sister.' My hairdresser suggested sending her a card. After having my hair done, off I went to buy a card. I wrote to her and apologised, 'If I have upset you in any kind of way, I will take the blame.' Which I always did. Peggy phoned the next day. 'Shall we meet tomorrow?' 'Yes!' I said. She came down the next day.

I couldn't believe what she said to me. Peggy said to me, 'You stopped me seeing my dying sister.' I wondered how? For six weeks I was ill, I was also on holiday for over two weeks. Then I was ill for another three weeks. What was stopping her seeing April? Peggy did not stop bellyaching. She had a go about my Rosie. 'Why didn't Rosie come over and tell me you were ill?' My Rosie that day drove from Southampton to Teignmouth, got a doctor for me, sorted me out, then drove to Reading, took Zoe to the doctor, then she had to drive back to Southampton. Can anyone see what we did wrong? I had to turn away from her. I think I could have slapped her across the face. She was behaving like a spoilt child. Wasn't my apology on the card good enough for her? Or did I need to lick her boots? I smiled at her and walked away. She caught up to me. 'Where shall we go?' Peggy said. As a black mood came over me, I thought, to hell and back.

I took all the family away for holidays in turn. Even Peggy. Paul would come down twice a year. We went to York. That was a really interesting holiday because there was so much to see. We did not fit in everything we wanted to see. Sometimes, Paul and I would just go to Exeter library, where they kept the old parish records. We were looking up the family tree. We found out a lot here, including the many different ways of spelling our surname. Sometimes, even in one family, we found four different way of spelling it. Another thing we discovered was that if they wanted the name, for example Charles, if the first born child dies, that name would be passed on to the next son that was born, and even the next son, as many as four times in one family. We didn't find this with the girls. We also went down to Cornwall, as that was where our ancestors had settled in the 1500s.

Every Monday we would skype each other and we would be on for over four hours, just talking about the family tree. We found Uncle Ted's children. I got in touch and invited them for a meal. It was lovely to meet them, Jane and Collin. We meet up a couple of times a year and enjoy each other's company. And Allen, known as Ted and his wife. Jane loved us meeting, as Uncle Ted had only married the year before me, so his children are about the same ages as my children. I had looked on Uncle Ted as my father since I had spent so much time with Gran. I told Jane all about the family and gave her a copy of the family tree.

I can't remember what order the holidays came in, or the years things happened. One year, Rosie joined Paul and me when we went to the Rhine Valley in Germany. That was a coach holiday. We had fun together, with lovely entertainment in the evening. Rosie and I went on another coach trip to Lake Garda. We met some lovely friends on this holiday. We went to Venice, Verona and the Dolomites.

Rosie and I love the sea, so we have done several cruises with P&O. Once we went to Barbados where we swam with the turtles. I was alright until one of the turtles swam under my tummy as I was on my way back to the boat. I didn't know they were that big! Rosie had the time of her life. Then Rosie went on a scuba dive. When she came back, she said, 'Mum, you missed a lovely sight. The fish were beautiful colours!' I am sorry that I can't swim like I used to. I have no strength in my left arm now. Then we went on to either St Lucia or St Martin, I am not sure. There was a big forest where the trees were very tall. We went in this cradle-like-thing and went up over the tops of the trees. Rosie and I were up in front, almost hanging over the bars, taking photos while the other people were clinging on to each other at the back. It reminded me of when we were children. We walked where angels fear to tread. We had a lovely time in the Caribbean. My holidays were invigorating with Rosie! She was so much more adventuresome and we spent so much time laughing.

183

When we got into the port of Gibraltar on one of our cruises, we took a boat trip to see the dolphins. Rosie was at the bow, taking photos when it started to get a bit rough. I put my camera away and Rosie got right in the bow. I put my arms right around her until I could hold the rails. Rosie got some lovely photos of the dolphins before one of the crew came down to check on us and see if we were alright. We said yes and she could see we were alright and that I was hanging on to Rosie and the rail.

On another cruise, though I can't remember where, we got on the boat in much deeper waters. It was very rough, but Rosie managed to get some very good shots of the whales. The only time *I* saw the dolphins was when I was being sick over them. The whole boat was being sick, including the crew! The boat was going from side to side and up and down. Rosie and I often chuckle over this. I guess, since the crew was sick as well, it must have been a tad rough!

Another time we went to Monaco. We had booked a trip while we were there, but it turned out there were only four of us. They sent a limo for us! We went up in a helicopter, all around the island. We could see our liner anchored in the bay. The trip in the helicopter was about half an hour, then back to the limo when we were then driven all around Monaco. We saw the little chapel where Prince Rainier and Princess Grace are laid to rest. We had a cup of tea and went into a little shop where we bought a few things. Then back to the ship. It was a lovely trip. On other cruises we went to Rome, Florence, the leaning Tower of Pisa, Portugal, Spain, Casablanca, Madeira and Barcelona.

Lydia just likes the U.K. Again, we have done a lot of different trips with Warner's Holidays because the food is very good, as is the evening entertainment. We went to the Isle of Wight, but Lydia always took our holiday in October or November, so everything I wanted to show her was closed. I was very disappointed about that since it is such a pretty place. We used to go to Birmingham a lot, to see Paul. Paul would stay at the hotel with us and we would do Christmas shopping. It was a nice opportunity for brother and sister to be together.

I also took Peggy, my sister, on a few holidays. One on the East Coast. The others I can't remember off hand. The ones I really remember were the last three. One was for her Birthday, the other was a Christmas present and the New Year. I just wouldn't leave her on her own. The first was Bodelwyddan Castle, a Warner holiday, for our birthdays. This was Peggy's birthday present from me. I had been to this place before, with Lydia. It was the Ritz's. It was a Majestic holiday, with trips included, so we went to Chester one day – Betws-y-coed.

52

On the day of my Birthday, November 2013, Peggy was not nice to me all day. She got the entertainment office to read something out for my birthday, but it was phrased in such a way that she got all the credit. She had the entertainment group come up and gave her hugs and kisses; not one said happy birthday to me, but it didn't worry me. She was only attention seeking as she told everyone she had a bad back. She got them eating out of her hand. What hurt me, was the smirk she gave me. She wanted to hurt me. I heard that the lady on the next table said, What a bitch! 'I hope you are not thinking about going home?' 'I've been toying with the idea,' I replied. 'Well, you're not! You are going to dance with us every night!' Peggy sat there like a sergeant major every evening. Her fan club would come around with hugs and kisses. She was still telling them about her bad back. The couple that sat bedside us asked me if she was paying for anything. 'No, this is my treat for her as it's her birthday,' I said. Soon, the holiday was over, and we were back in Teignmouth.

The bad back disappeared. The next day we met up with one of Peggy's friends and went in for a coffee. Peggy was boasting about what she had done on my birthday, to the amazement of her friends, and she went on with her story, laughing her head off, thinking it was funny, her friend looked at me with pity in her eyes. In a few days we were off again, this time to the Isle of Wight. It was Christmas 2013. My Paul was coming with us on this holiday, but Peggy had borrowed one of my walking sticks to make her story more authentic. She really put on a good act this time.

As soon as we were out of Teignmouth, out came the stick. Peggy got friendly with a couple from Exeter. They sat with her throughout the holiday. I played bingo with them every evening, even though I didn't like bingo; I was just being sociable. Then, one evening, Peggy told me that her new friend was giving her a pound short every night. 'Well, make her get her own tickets or ask for the money!' I said. 'I don't like to,' said Peggy. 'Bigger fool you then!' I replied. I walked back to our table. It could have been Peggy trying to get more money out of me. I was not biting!

I could see this new friend of Peggy's didn't like me. Paul was quite friendly with the woman's husband which I was pleased about. I just kept Paul topped up with drinks. He didn't drink much. I said, 'Do you mind if I go on the dance floor?' Paul said, 'Go ahead; enjoy yourself, Mum.' Well, I wasn't wanted at the table, by the feel of it, so I started dancing on my own like most of the women were doing. That is, until this Welshman saw me. He asked me, 'Do you mind if I join you?' 'Lovely!' I said, and we danced together the whole of the holiday. It was on this holiday that the trouble started. Peggy hadn't brought enough jumpers with her and she asked if she could borrow one of mine. I said she could, as I had plenty with me.

I opened the drawer and took them out and put them on the bed. Peggy tried on a couple. They didn't fit, as I was a good size smaller than Peggy at this time. Then she spotted the only one I didn't want her to have, for sentimental reasons. It was given to me by a good friend who had died, and every time I touched it, I could see my friend's smiling face and remember the lovely time we had together. Peggy said, 'You're not getting this back! It fits me better than you; I am going to keep it. A flash of our younger days came back … when Mum would say 'Peggy can wear any of yours'. 'I want it back, Peggy; it's only on loan.' She just walked out of the room. I called for Paul and went down to dinner. Peggy joined us. It was rather quiet at dinner. Peggy couldn't get out to her new friends quick enough. 'Look at this lovely jumper! It was my sister's but it's mine now.' I said, 'It's not yours! It's on loan. It's mine. Please return it at the end of the evening.' I thank the Welshman for making my holiday so nice in the evenings. He was a very nice gent, but we never exchanged names.

We got back to Newton Abbot. Peggy said, 'I will run on and get the taxi.' 'Why? Are you paying for it?' I asked. 'No,' she said. 'I don't have any money! I said, 'Paul and I are getting the train!' Peggy's face said everything. I was getting fed up being taken for granted. She never bought me so much as a cup of tea or a drink in the evening, on all three holidays. I had to put my hand in my pocket for every lunch we had out on the trips and all the little extras, right down to her ticket to get back to Teignmouth. I went to buy the tickets.

Peggy began to run backwards and forwards, pulling her big case towards a bus. There was no sign of a bad back or stick! 'Hurry up! The bus is waiting for us,' she said. I wondered what Peggy was talking about. The ticket man had just told me next train to Teignmouth was from platform three.

There were big notices all over the station: if anyone needed to go to Totnes, Plymouth or Cornwall, they needed to get the bus outside the station to Totnes as there was work being done on the lines between Newton Abbot and Totnes. I shouted to Peggy, 'Paul and I are going to platform three. If you want to get on the bus, do so!' Honestly, Peggy was like an idiot, running up and down, pulling a big case behind her all the time. We got back to Teignmouth, no thanks to Peggy. Then Peggy said, 'We will go up Shute Hill. I wasn't keen on going up this way as it was very steep. I was thinking about Paul, as he was getting over deep vein thrombosis and I know how much that hurts, having had it myself.

Peggy was up the top of Shute Hill, with Paul and me a long way behind. When we finally reached the top, I found I had dropped my mp3 player. I went back to where my bag had slipped off the case and found it. I soon got back to Paul. 'Where is my case?' I asked. 'Aunty Peggy took it!' So, Peggy had pulled two heavy cases from Shute Hill to Fore Street, a good ten minutes down the road. I took my case and said thank you to Peggy, but I felt like saying, 'I see your back's better!' Paul and I walked to the flat. Two blissful days without Peggy.

But I had to take Peggy on one last holiday. In my heart I didn't want to. How could I renege on my promise to give her these three holidays for her birthday and Christmas presents? She still made this holiday unpleasant. Maybe she thought I didn't spend enough money on her. The three holidays for her cost over one thousand six hundred; it was always dear at that time of the year. Plus, all the extras. The evening before, Peggy phoned to ask what time we were leaving the next day. I told her the taxi would get us at half past six in the morning and would take us up to Eastcliff. We had to be there by seven a.m. Off we went to the Chatsworth Hotel in Llandudno, to see in the New Year, 2014.

Peggy sat by me again, moaning and groaning constantly. She got up out of her seat, making so much fuss and then brought the stick back out again. Then she sat in the seat again. We stopped again for a comfort stop and Peggy started her moaning and groaning again. I couldn't help it and said, in a sarcastic voice, 'You poor old dear! Do you want me to help you up?' Peggy said in a very loud voice, 'You would groan if you had a bad back like mine!' Then this chap in front of me gave me a dirty look every time he passed me throughout the holiday. Still in my sarcastic voice I said, 'Thanks a bunch, Peggy. I am now the wicked sister. Oh no, let me get that right! I am the ugly wicked sister!' People were looking at me as if I had gone mad. I just couldn't care less anymore. With her attention seeking, Peggy was out to spoil another holiday.

I got our drinks and told Peggy she could sit in Paul's seat as he was leaving the day after we got home. I wanted to spend a little time with him. I did not want Peggy to spoil what little time I would have with Paul this holiday. We got to the hotel and usually walked up the stairs as the lift was nearly always full. Peggy ran up the stairs to get the kettle on. Paul and I plodded up behind. By the time we reached the room, I could hardly breathe and had to sit down. So did Paul who was no better than me. Peggy almost had the kettle boiled by the time we got to the room. She got nasty. 'I am only here to make the tea!' You could see she meant it. (That would have been an expensive cuppa!) I turned around and said, 'Peggy, if you had given me a chance to get my breath back, I would have made the tea. I am not lazy. If you like, throw it down the sink. I will do Paul's and mine in my own time.' 'It's done now!' said Peggy.

Next day, I was having one of my bad turns (atrial fibrillation). I went down to breakfast with Paul. I had a cup of tea and he had a good cooked breakfast. Peggy joined us. I said to Paul, 'Do you want some money to do some shopping for yourself, down in the town? Or you can sit in the bedroom and watch TV which won't disturb me.' Paul said, 'I'll stay with you Mum.' Peggy said, 'I will stay as well.' I just lay down and went to sleep.' The next thing I knew, Paul was waking me up saying it was time to go down to lunch.

We were going to have lunch before going to the pantomime in the afternoon. I had a cup of tea and Paul had something to eat. I could have done without this, but for Paul I made the effort. I didn't want to spoil things for him. I don't know if Paul guessed I was not well, but he seemed to stay very close to me. I could see he didn't like the way Aunty Peggy was behaving towards me. He just sat next to me and held my hand. I think I slept through most of the pantomime! The coach was waiting outside for us and took us back to the hotel again. When we got back Paul told me to go and have a rest saying that he would call me on the way to dinner. I went to my room and fell asleep yet again. That evening, I felt a lot better; the AF was passing.

I forgot to say that, when Peggy went to sit in Paul's seat on the coach, she met up with three Welsh ladies. Peggy was quite thick with them. The chap who sat in front of me was still giving me dirty looks. In the end, I stopped this chap and his wife, 'What are all the dirty looks for? What have I done to you?' He said, 'For the way you spoke to your sister.' I replied, 'This is an act with her; she is attention seeking. If you followed her off the coach, you would see her running up the back stairs. I took her away in November, for a birthday again, for Christmas to the Isle of Wight, and I now brought her here. She has made me ill with stress and I just can't take any more. She has spoiled all three holidays.' My sister does not have a bad back! She just likes to make out that I am the wicked sister.' The wife spoke up, turning to her husband, 'I told you so and you wouldn't believe me!' I said, 'Yes! This is only the tip of the iceberg. It has been ongoing since our childhood. But coming up in the coach, I am sorry, I just snapped!' The chap took my hand, shook it and said, 'I am very, very sorry. But she is good actress! She took me in. We could nominate her for a Oscar!' and we all laughed.

53

That evening was the Old-Year's-out, New-Year's-in party. Everyone seemed to be having fun. Most of us were dancing and having a good time but you wouldn't believe what happened next. The three Welsh ladies got up to dance. Peggy hobbled over on her stick and stopped the ladies dancing in the middle of the dance floor to tell them about her bad back. I take it that was what she was doing, as she was rubbing her back. I don't think the ladies were impressed, as they soon started to dance again. I think the Welsh ladies put the evil eye on her! As she hobbled back to our table and sat down, this other lady stood up and knocked my drink all over Peggy. She hobbled her way out of the room to change.

Peggy came back in dressed in a lovely expensive dress I had given her. She thought it was too low, so I had bought her a silk vest top to go underneath. Instead of the silk vest, Peggy had put two big safety pins in front which looked ridiculous. She was trying to make herself look like orphan Annie. That dress cost ninety pounds back in the nineties. I only wore it once and I had dropped a dress size, so it was now too big for me and I had given it to Peggy. Everyone was looking at her and laughing behind her back. I think she should definitely have had an Oscar for best actress this time.

One more day, then we were to go home. That day, I took Paul out shopping to make sure he had everything he needed to go home with. Paul was going back the day after we got back to Teignmouth. On the last night there, our group decided that we had really enjoyed each other's company and we all planned to meet up there again at the end of 2014 to see the next New Year in. But, without Peggy. I would never take her on another holiday.

When we got home the next day Peggy came around. She said, 'I have come for my Christmas present, from Paul.' My Paul was still in bed. I knocked at his door, 'Paul, Aunty Peggy is here for her Christmas present!' I said. 'In here, Mum.' I went into Paul's room and he gave it to me to give to Aunty Peggy. She never thanked him. She was holding a bag and wacked me in the tummy with it, and then she was gone. No goodbyes! Nothing! I thought she might have brought my jumper back, but no luck. In the bag were the heated hair roller tongs and the Abba suit I had bought her for the sixties night at the Alice Cross a long time ago. Why she gave it back to me, I don't know. It was no good for me now. It was far too big, so I passed it on to someone else.

Why didn't Peggy tell me she was off to America for three months to see her daughter and two grandsons? Although I knew Peggy was going to America at some point when we got back, I had other things on my mind. While we were away, I was busy making sure Paul was kitted out and had everything to go back with. Peggy told Madge, her friend next door, that she had phoned me, but I was in all day. I didn't hear the phone. Peggy didn't return my jumper. I was very cross with her. Because Mum had allowed Peggy to use anything of mine, this brought back bad memories. I felt I needed to stop her. What else would she covet and take of mine if I didn't. She knew taking that jumper was going to hurt me.

This is when I wrote the first letter to Peggy. Somehow, she managed to use the letter to turn one of my nephews against me. I might have gone a little over the top, but not enough for that. I finally got my jumper back. Though very misshapen. Peggy had taken it to America. I don't know if she gave it to her daughter, or her daughter took it from Peggy's things she kept over in America. But her daughter had been wearing it. When I tried it on, it was like a dress on me. Ann is a good size twenty-six (Plus---s), and me a size ten. Being woollen, I thought I would try and shrink it, so I put it in hot water. That shrunk it a bit, but not nearly enough, so I tried again. I got it down a little more, I would have said about a size eighteen, but if I tried it again, I would spoil it. I knew it was never going to fit me again and I didn't want the jumper anymore. It felt full of hate, so I gave it to Lydia. That was late 2014. I took Paul, Lydia and Rosie on their yearly holidays. We had a lovely time and so enjoyed each other's company.

Then Paul and I went back for the New Year reunion in Llandudno and had a lovely time. There was a lady there who wanted to adopt Paul! I said, 'No way! They asked, 'Where's Peggy this year?' I pulled a face. 'What? Are trying for the Oscar, this year? Peter said. 'I was so creased over Peggy I had to go outside when she came

192

down with those two great safety pins stuck in her dress!' I said, 'Peggy is very modest!' 'Why didn't she just put chain mail armour on instead?' said Peter. His wife, Janet, said, 'It was a pretty dress!' 'It was mine,' I said. 'My husband had bought it for me for a party and so I only wore it for a few hours. I dropped a dress size, but I couldn't bring myself to part with it. I thought when we went on the three holidays that Peggy needed some evening clothes. Like a fool, I gave it to her and that is what she did to it!'

We had a lovely time seeing the New Year 2015 in. We will keep in touch. I haven't seen Peggy for over a year. Things have come back to me over the years. Peggy had changed doctors, so she didn't bump into me, and at the whist club she was boasting that if she saw me coming, she would go into a shop, or up an alley, to hide from me. Why? Am I going to hit her over the head with my stick or something? It just doesn't make sense. I forgave her as I have at other times. She is my sister, and I still love her. I have tried sending her birthday cards, but she puts them back through the letter box with a nasty note on the back.

In 2015, my heart condition got worse, so I needed an ultra-sound, which came up with leaky valves. The pump is not working too well, which gives me shortness of breath and makes me a little light-headed from time to time which has slowed me down a lot. It also stopped me doing some of things I love to do, like dancing and walking. I also get the odd angina attack, but I kept going. Paul was still coming down at Easter time and Christmas. We would go away sometimes. Paul and I would Skype most Mondays and talk about the family tree. I would go out with friends sometimes, for holidays, out for meals, or coffee up the Alice Cross and the Woman's Fellowship at the Baptist Church most Sundays. We must not forget our holidays with Lydia and Rosie, which I wrote about earlier and some of the placcs we visited.

54

2016 was more or less the same, but Christmas of that year I thought I would put out a hand of friendship to Peggy as Tim, her husband, was moving to a new nursing home. Now Tim and I had been friends from a very young age when we all went swimming down the Quay. They named our little bunch The Quay Rats. Every year Tim was in the nursing home I sent him birthday cards and Christmas cards. I didn't know the address of the new nursing home, so I sent a Christmas card to Tim for Peggy to give to him, and also a Christmas card to Peggy. I received a horrific letter from Peggy, about Sid, when he had left me destitute over fifty years earlier. It was hard enough living through that time. I got very depressed about all the lies Peggy wrote in the letter.

I will forgive Peggy for saying I tried to committed suicide, as this came from my Mum, as this is what my Mum had said when she was trying take my children away from me. We know now that Mum was only after the money. All I was doing, in my state of mind, at that time, was to feed my children. If there was anything left over, I fed myself.

I never dumped my children on Peggy. She was living in a one bed flat in the Triangle at that time. She had just had Dora. As I said before, my April had the children in the school holidays, as I didn't want Mum and Peggy to know Sid had left me destitute. And I can prove some of this. Peggy never came to the hospital like she said, as she had a young baby at that time. The other thing she wrote about Roger throwing me out was also not true. Rosie, Robin and I went to a battered wives' home, then I asked Peggy if she could put us up for a few days since she was in a bigger house by this time. This was a while before going home. It would do the children good to relax on the beach for a few days and then we went home.

I can prove most of what Peggy wrote was lies. Why did she bring up things that happened over fifty years ago? Just because I sent them two Christmas cards. I am beginning to think Peggy is sick. It comes back through a friend of Peggy's, that if I apologise for hurting her, she will come back into my life. I have forgiven her, but I won't apologise, as the same thing will happen again. Why has she got to keep on hurting me? Please, someone! Tell me!

From 2017, I just got on with my life with the help of friends. I have made very good friends here in Teignmouth and have a full life. My children come to stay with me, and I know they love me. Rosie comes down from Southampton to do my heavy shopping, making sure I have enough to eat. She has done this ever since I have lived in Teignmouth. I have got good friends here at the Alice Cross and the Baptist Church. If I am honest, I do not miss Peggy in my life. If she is happy where she is, I am happy where I am. But I did say to my children, 'If you want to see Aunty Peggy any time, please do. She is your Aunty. What goes on between your Aunty and me is nothing to do with you children.' But I must say, if I have heard Peggy has not been well, or something has gone wrong, I asked Lydia over to see Aunty Peggy if I have been able to. I would help Peggy and never turn my back on her.

In my later years I have taken my religion seriously, as I did in my early days, as my sins weighed heavily on me. I asked Jamie, our Minister, if he would baptize me. My Baptism took place at the Baptist Church on the twenty third of October 2016. As I stepped down into the water, Jamie and Bill were at my side. I went under the water, and as Jamie and Bill pulled me up, I felt as if a weight was taken off me. My friend Ruth was there, ready to wrap the towel around me. This is when my Rosie turned to me and told me, 'When your times comes, you should now have a Church funeral. So, I have changed my funeral plans and they will take place at the Baptist Church with my Baptist family.

55

It is now 2018. This was one of the saddest times of my life. Every year, I would take Paul somewhere for his birthday. Rosie wanted to come this time, so we decided on Cardiff. But it had to be earlier this year, as Rosie needed to use her leave up by March. I sent Paul the money for his fare to come down to Cardiff. I booked up the hotel and Rosie was going to drive us up. The day we had planned to go, down came the snow. It was heavy, so I phoned a friend, to see if Rosie could park her car there. Rosie and I went by train instead.

We had a lovely time in Cardiff and went to Cardiff Castle. There was a lot to see there. Then we went down in the tunnels. Apparently, a lot of the Cardiff people took cover here during the air raids, so they had a mock-up there. It was as if you were back in the war, in the middle of an air raid. It bought back vivid memories because it was so realistic. It took me back to my childhood, holding on to my brother and sister, with our Vera Lynn singing in the background. It bought tears to my eyes as I sang along. We found a very good restaurant, so we ate there every evening, but the weather was bitter. We did some shopping and I gave Paul some more money for his birthday in April. He needed a new printer as he was going to do some printing for me on the family tree.

That was the last I saw of Paul. On 6th June 2018 my Paul died. It was a bitter blow to me as he played a big part in my life. I asked Lydia, if I bought a rose, would she put Paul's ashes in her garden. She said no. She said that she could throw the ashes in the chicken pen for the chickens to scratch over. I couldn't believe what she had just said. It was like putting a knife through my heart. After all, it was her brother. I know we Christians believe the body is only a carcass that carries the soul, and that the soul goes on to heaven or hell. But it was Paul's body that carried that soul, and it should be treated with respect. Jamie, our Minister came up and said a few words to bring us closer. We sang a hymn and his ashes ended up in a beautiful little glade by a steam, with the birds singing, in France. We thought it was such a pretty spot for a very loving son and brother. 'Farewell, my loving Son.'

What we were doing over in France, was paying tribute to my Uncle Walter, who died in the first world war. When I came back from France, my ambition was to put a show on at Alice Cross to celebrate the Centenary of the end of the First World War, 1914-1918 and the Centenary of The R.A.F. The remembrance of all the men who had Fallen. All the proceeds were to be split between the Alice Cross and SSAFA, a military charity. The first on board was my lovely friend Effie. Without her help, I might had fallen by the wayside. She was at my side, giving me sound advice the whole time. But she wouldn't take any of the credit.

We wanted the audience to play a part. I compiled song sheets, so that they could join in with the singing. To start off the show they sang songs from the first and second world wars. Then I got people from the Alice Cross who could sing and dance, and they were all willing to join in. They were very supportive. I even sang two songs myself. We had the audience taking part again, with more rousing songs. To see all the happy faces all waving their flags, brought me near to tears.

Now we are coming to the close of another year, by joining the friends at the Alice Cross for Christmas Dinner with the Baptist Church. I couldn't wish for nicer people to be with. 'Thank you, all.'

At the start of 2019, I knew I had another lump in my other breast. What was I going to do if it was cancer again? I couldn't tell anyone, so I kept it to myself. I took one of my nieces on holiday and I still couldn't say anything. As time went on, I carried on keeping it to myself. My heart was in my mouth. To top it all off, my heart started to play up. Where do I go from here? I had such a bad time with the cancer last time. Am I strong enough to go through it again this time? On my own, in July, I picked up the phone and phoned the doctor.

The doctor said, 'Come in to see me.' So, off I went. It was a new doctor. I told her about the trouble with my heart, and she was going to arrange for me to have a test. I don't know what it was about that doctor, but I was able to blurt out that I had a lump in my right breast. She examined my right breast. 'We'd better sort this out first and sort your heart out later.' By the 9th July 2019, it was confirmed the cancer was back. By the 25th of July, I was having my pre-operative talk I then I had to go for a pre-assessment.

On the 2nd August 2019, I went in for day-surgery. Mary came with me each time. She has always been with me each time I have needed to go to hospital since coming back to Teignmouth. She has been a really true friend. Even when Paul died, it was Mary who took over. Now she was joined by Rosie, as Rosie had come down to look after me for four days. Bless her! Then Lydia came up for a couple of days. I had to go to Torbay hospital. Then I was put on tablets for the next five years.

They are preparing me for radiotherapy in October, for three weeks. Monday to Friday. Fifteen days. In all this, my Baptist friends have stepped in. I have been so blessed with friends at this time. Rosie is going to take me up to see her daughter, my granddaughter, for a few days, which will make a nice break. Then Lydia will be up for a few days before radiotherapy.

56

I needed to put this story in writing. The good *and* the bad. While writing my memoir, things have become so alive and so very vivid. Sometimes it would make me laugh and sometimes made me cry as it was so painful. I have not found it easy to write this memoir, as it has opened old wounds and I have told you my darkest secrets. The mistakes I made in my life, like giving up my house, when my first marriage fell apart. To go up to Mum's, as I didn't want to marry Roger or Ed. I was just weak. It wasn't for sex. With Roger it was to keep a roof over my children's heads. Ed was my biggest mistake, as it was to keep Roger at bay, as I was afraid of taking him back, as he was so ill. But, my Robin came first.

Philip was never a mistake. He turned out to be my one true love. That man *did* love me and in turn I loved him. There are still a lot of unanswered questions like, did my Mum ever love me? As a child my Mum knocked my confidence badly for years. I thought I was an ugly duckling. I still lack confidence to this day, though I put a brave face on things. Mum would play us children one off against the other. But I am still very grateful to Mum. She worked hard to keep a roof over our heads and food on the table. It couldn't have been easy for her in those days. There was no N.H.S. and no handouts.

I do know that it was partly Mum's fault that Dad left. Mum was too hard on him. And Dad was too soft, like me in 1954 when I had enough. I ran like Dad and when Dad married the second time, they had a child and Dad stayed until the day he died. But still I am very grateful to Mum, as she kept us together as a family. I knew my brothers and sisters, and the bond us three older children had, was never broken. So, I shall always love my Mum and my siblings. We are family. Good or bad.

'Please forgive us, God, for all our sins and take care of our dear departed souls.'

Printed in Poland
by Amazon Fulfillment
Poland Sp. z o.o., Wrocław

61223935R00112